THE SATISFIED LIFE

Jane McAvoy

THE SATISFIED LIFE

Medieval Women Mystics on Atonement

The Pilgrim Press
Cleveland, Ohio

The Pilgrim Press, Cleveland, Ohio 44115
© 2000 by Jane McAvoy

Grateful acknowledgment for permission to reprint the following:
From *Hildegard of Bingen*, translated by Mother Columba Hart and Jane Bishop,
© 1990 by the Abbey of Regina Laudis: Benedictine Congregation
Regina Laudis of the Strict Observance, Ind. Used by permission of Paulist Press.
✷ From *Mechthild of Magdeburg*, translated and introduced by Frank Tobin, © 1998
by Frank Tobin. Used by permission of Paulist Press.

Printed in the United States of America on acid-free paper

05 04 03 02 01 00   5 4 3 2 1

Library of Congress Cataloging-in-Publication Data

McAvoy, Jane Ellen, 1957–
    The satisfied life : medieval women mystics on atonement / Jane McAvoy.
    p. cm.
    Includes bibliographical references (p.) and index.
    ISBN 0-8298-1377-2 (paper : alk. paper)
        1. Atonement—History of doctrines—Middle Ages, 600–1500. 2. Women
mystics—Europe. 3. Feminist theology. I. Title.

BT263 .M28 2000
232'.3—dc21
                                                            99-054447

To Greg

CONTENTS

✳

PREFACE

his book began in classes at Hiram College, where I
found the work of medieval women mystics to be an
entry point for questions about gender, culture, and
the study of religion. My students were often fasci-
nated by and attracted to the strange world of the
Middle Ages, and they found in the women they stud-
ied support and challenge for their own life journeys.
When I was granted a sabbatical by Hiram College in the winter of 1997,
the writings of medieval women mystics had taken hold of me and I settled
down to figure out what, if anything, they had to say to contemporary
Christians. During Lent of that year I was asked to prepare a lecture for seminary students at Lexington Theological Seminary. I decided atonement was
an appropriate theme. Julian of Norwich's parable of the lord and servant was
foremost in my consciousness. It was then that I realized that her vision of
God's unconditional love is a meaningful model of atonement that directly
challenges Anselm's theology of satisfaction. Julian is the basis for a new
understanding of satisfaction that speaks in a unique way to the concerns of
feminist theology and the realities of contemporary Christians.

This project is the enlargement of that insight into a feminist theology of
atonement. The thesis of this book is that atonement is the good news that
we are saved by the satisfying love of God. Students of reformation era theology know that Luther's insight was that righteousness is an action of God,

not an attribute of God. We are made righteous by God. In a similar manner, I will argue that satisfaction is the work of God, brought to us in the life, death, and resurrection of Jesus Christ. It is a work that heals the world, makes us whole, and propels Christians to meaningful lives of searching, serving, and suffering. The Christian gospel envisions the satisfied life.

The book is divided into two parts. The first strives to outline the ontology of atonement. Beginning with a basic discussion of atonement as satisfaction, it defines the nature of the problem of humanity and the corresponding saving work of God. Questions about how we respond to that saving work both in relation to God and in relation to the world complete this section. The second section of the work discusses three medieval women who, each in her own way, lived a satisfied life. Studying their lives helps us to understand further how we might put the idea of the satisfied life into practice. From this combination of theoretical and practical reflection emerges a dense description of the satisfied life that can inform and challenge our journeys in faith.

My own journey in faith has been opened up to new insights about the Christian life. I now understand the process of salvation as a holistic endeavor. It is not a choice between the incarnation and the crucifixion as the moment of salvation, or of objective theories or subjective theories of atonement as the method of theological reflection. Salvation is about being in love with God and with God's creation. The blood that births Jesus and flows from the cross is part of the flow of love that is the being of God in the world. Our lives are part of this flow of love, and the more we realize this, the more satisfying is the reality of our salvation. When we dare to think anew about the theology of atonement, we are standing in the company of Christian women who were committed to the Christian community and were able to make the ageless claim of salvation in Christ meaningful in their own day. It is my earnest hope that this study will make a modest contribution to the meaning of salvation in our day.

In addition to Hiram College, which generously supported my research with faculty grants and a semester sabbatical, I am grateful to the Disciples Divinity House at Vanderbilt University for giving my husband and me housing and hospitality during my sabbatical. While I was at Vanderbilt, Jane Barr allowed me to sit in on her class on the study of Christian women and to present my ideas about Julian of Norwich. My current colleagues at Lexington Theological Seminary have given me encouragement to continue my work. I am thankful for my research assistants Brandon Gilvin, Kitty Roark, Lori Smallwood, and Sami Wilson. Lectures at Eastern Kentucky University, Hiram College, and Lexington Theological Seminary helped me work out the ontology of satisfaction. The Louisville Institute supplied funding for the completion of Part Two of this work. My friends in the Association of Disciples for Theological Discussion listened to a first draft of chapter 5. William Barr, Deborah Core, Lucinda Huffaker, William Paulsell, and Stephen Webb made suggestions that helped me think through my reflections. Behind the scenes, my friends Sandra Parker and Joyce Dyer listened with interest to my ideas. In the classroom, the earnest desire of my students for new answers to old questions kept me working. Quite a few years ago it was a class with Bernard McGinn that first inspired my desire to study women mystics. I am grateful for the support of Timothy Staveteig, as well as the rest of the staff at The Pilgrim Press, who understood the character and direction of my writing. At home, my husband, Greg Russell, kept me going and always reminded me to practice what I preach. This book is dedicated to him for his support of my work and for his abiding love.

✖ ✖ ✖

ACHIEVING
SELF-SATISFACTION

W e live in an era obsessed with self-development and success. Go to any bookstore and you will find that the fastest-growing section is self-help. Whether it's Rick Pitino's recent book, *Success Is a Choice: 10 Steps to Overachieving in Business and Life,* or Louise Hay's *You Can Heal Your Life,* the promise is that the right book—the right approach to life—can save us from our problems. Through discipline, hard work, and sacrifice we can reach happiness and personal satisfaction. This leads to an interesting question: Does satisfaction come through sacrifice?

Theologically, we call this atonement, often understood as "at-one-ment." Christians assume that the path to personal satisfaction has something to do with Jesus Christ, who overcomes whatever it is that keeps us from being satisfied. It is an idea that is attracting new interest in theology because it cuts to the heart of Christian belief and tries to make sense of the meaning of sin, salvation, and the work of Christ as it relates to our experience of life. Thus it is a relational and experiential concept that addresses three key theological questions: What are we saved from? What are we saved for? Who or what are we saved by? The first question addresses the nature of sin. The second envisions the goal of salvation for ourselves and for the world. The third explores the meaning of the work of God in Christ.

The problem is how to make sense of this third question. The stumbling block, as the apostle Paul would say, is the meaning of the death of Christ. Traditionally, theories of atonement have rested on the importance of Christ's sacrificial death as the means of human salvation. Yet, as Pamela Dickey Young notes, this idea of Jesus' death as salvific leads to some troubling thoughts about the nature of God's action and the corresponding human response:

> How then are we to make sense of a religious tradition that has often been seen to focus itself on the cruel and untimely death of its central figure? . . . A tradition wherein the father sits silently by or condones or even wills the death of a son appears as "divine child abuse" rather than as saving act. . . . To see Jesus' suffering as redemptive has been taken in the history of the tradition to suggest that this suffering is an example to be imitated by the faithful.[1]

These troubling reflections get at the heart of feminist critiques of atonement theology. In 1973 Mary Daly argued that the theology of atonement reinforces the scapegoat syndrome for women, because it implies that it is somehow natural to imitate Christ's suffering. More recently, womanist theologian Delores Williams has shown how ideas of atonement reinforce the negative history of African American women's surrogacy. Speaking from the perspective of liberation theology, Mary Solberg argues that any theology that tries to reinterpret the value of suffering is not liberating to the victims of servitude or violence, but rather is concerned with protecting God and those who benefit from the suffering of others. Therefore, feminist theologians such as Joanne Carlson Brown suggest that the best course is just to do away with the idea of atonement because theology cannot offer redemption while perpetuating devaluation.[2]

I question the value of this dismissive approach. I agree that theology cannot be redemptive while reinforcing oppression. However, by denouncing atonement as a nonredemptive theological doctrine, we have given up on the good news that we do not save ourselves. Without a doctrine of atonement, we are left with the conclusion that we are responsible for our own salvation. The problem is thinking that our presence, our suffering on behalf of others, will make everything all right. It is not only socially sanctioned for women to sacrifice for others. It is the epitome of Christian practice.

The contemporary theologian Roberta Bondi confesses that the message she received from Christianity is that the formula for salvation does not save. What Christianity taught her is that sin plus love plus sacrifice equals salvation. The sin of our corrupted will is only overcome by the sacrificial love of Christ and of all those who would follow him. Having spent her life studying church history, she knew this formula was not true. The earliest Christian theologians stressed that sin is a deep internal woundedness, which is overcome by the healing love of God. Despite this knowledge, she could not believe in the grace of this healing love because it upset everything she knew about her relationship with God, with her husband, her father, her mother, herself. What she knew in her head was that salvation does not come through sacrificial love. What she believed in her heart, and more importantly lived out in her life, was that through sacrifice she could make people love her. The conclusion was that self-sacrifice was not only natural, but divinely ordained.

The horror of this understanding of self-sacrifice was revealed to her in a dream. She imagined her husband kneeling by the bathtub, his neck held under a drain while a powerful-looking man with a huge knife threatened to kill her. "Don't hurt her," her husband said. "Take me instead." In horror she watched as the killer slit her husband's throat. She was stunned by the graphic brutality of this act of sacrificial love and horrified by the realization that this act of cruel violence had been taught to her as the foundation of Christian faith. As she woke up, she declared, "This is what you've always thought the crucifixion is about, but this is not it."[3]

Bondi reminds us that theology happens in a cultural context. It is not enough to know the history of Christian theology. It has to be integrated into present experience. When the message of sacrificial love is preached in a world where we are surrounded by violence and where women are taught that sacrifice can appease the wrath of others, the result is that our imagination is captured by a perversion of the message of salvation. Like Bondi, most of us assume we know this is not really the Christian gospel, yet at the deepest levels of our Christian lives we experience a cognitive dissonance that can paralyze our faith.

It is especially crucial for those who lead the Christian community to reflect on the meaning of atonement. There are many women and men who find satisfaction in the role of ministry and want to celebrate their growing service to the church. This means taking a leadership role in the central moment of worship, communion. And increasingly, ministers informed by the feminist criticism of atonement are realizing the conflict between the liberating sense of calling that has brought them to this new role and the theology of communion that glorifies violent sacrifice. This question is intensified by the current backlash to feminist theology, which has argued that criticism of atonement is equal to heresy.[4] At a recent conference, women ministers urged me to help them make sense out of sacrifice, both Christ's and their own, so that they could figure out how to celebrate Christ's death and resurrection in a life-enriching rather than a life-denying manner. For the sake of these leaders and all Christians, there is a desperate need to reclaim a sense of the liberating grace of God in the work of Jesus Christ.

Theologians have responded to the feminist critique of atonement theology in a number of ways. The more conservative approach is to suggest that feminists have missed the point. Atonement is not about a sacrifice to appease God's wrath, but a way of life that preserves social order. Therefore all we need to do is return to the true meaning of traditional theories. Another approach is to suggest that feminists have a point, but there is a difference between abusive use of atonement theology and atonement as abusive. The solution is to highlight lesser-known theories of atonement from the Christian tradition such as those of Abelard or Irenaeus. Feminist and womanist theologians are more likely to take a different route. Delores Williams suggests returning to the Scriptures, especially the Synoptic Gospels, which she argues are the basis for a theology that centers on Jesus' life, not death. Mary Grey is a bit more radical, and bases a theology of redemption on women's experience of mothering rather than on scripture or tradition.[5]

While there is some merit in all these approaches, in this work we will explore unused sources from the Christian tradition that were written by medieval women, in an attempt to uncover the value of their alternative theories of atonement. Such sources can draw us out of our own subjectivity to see things anew. To get inside a source from the Christian tradition is a valuable tool in forming our own theology. At those points where a source from the tradition confirms our ideas, we can claim a precedent for our theology. At those places where we are challenged by the otherness of tradition, we can be drawn out of the prejudices or inconsistencies in our own lives. The task is not to live in the past but to think through how the past can illumine our vision of the present.

However, the use of Scripture alone as the source of Christian tradition is problematic because there is no complete theory of atonement in Scripture.

In essence, one has to justify the selection and interpretation of Scripture, and that leads either back to experience or forward to sources from Christian history. Since there is no one theory of atonement in Scripture, theologians have constructed a variety of types of atonement theologies, which have been accepted as valid forms of Christian faith. Paul Fiddes, for example, argues that we need different models of atonement for the different types of people in the world. Since we live in a shared historical context, we can also argue that certain types of atonement theology may be particularly suited to a certain age.[6]

A few theologians have begun the work of retrieving models of atonement from the Christian tradition. Fiddes himself argues for a retrieval of Abelard's theory of atonement as a moral influence that shows us the virtue of self-sacrificial love. However, this approach is not particularly suited to a feminist context that contends that self-sacrifice is the problem rather than the solution. More recently, Darby Ray has suggested looking back to patristic sources that emphasize atonement as ushering in a realm of justice.[7] While themes of justice are suited to our age and the concerns of a feminist audience, this approach still does not address the problem at the root of Bondi's experience—the nature of saving love. (Bondi herself hints that she finds solace in patristic sources, but never outlines a model of atonement based on these sources.)

An atonement theology that responds to the feminist critique will need to articulate the nature of saving love and a vision of a just world redeemed by this love. It will be a theology that is informed by women's experience and that desires to speak to the reality of all human experience and strives to articulate a theology for contemporary Christian men as well as women. Theologies that reinforce notions of abusive love will be critiqued as inadequate not just for women but for the whole world. At the same time, a feminist articulation of atonement will be considered as a meaningful model, particularly for those who have struggled with the nature of saving love and long to break free from the language of abuse.

A theology based on women's writing is particularly suited to respond to the feminist critique of abuse and has the added bonus of allowing one to incorporate feminist hermeneutics of analysis concerning the unique problems and possibilities of writing in a woman's voice. One of these problems and possibilities is the form of women's writing. The vast majority of women in Christian history were barred from formal training for theological writing, so they wrote down their ideas about Christian faith in the form of letters, visions, prayer manuals, and spiritual autobiographies. Since these writings discuss the mystery of experiencing God, they are referred to as mystical texts.

While there is some question whether these mystical texts can be adequate sources for theological reflection, they are beginning to gain credibility as real theology. Bernard McGinn has noted that those who would dismiss mystical writing as inadequate for theological reflection have only proven the narrowness of their own understanding of theology.[8] He calls mystical writing vernacular theology. Women mystics are especially prone to write in the vernacular (the native language) rather than Latin and to use literary forms that merge theological concepts and religious experience. As such they are a rich resource for the very kind of authentic theology that Bondi argues we need in order to integrate what we know to be true with what we really believe. Mystical theology provides the possibility of addressing the objective reality of being saved by God while highlighting the subjective experience of salvation.

The bulk of these mystical writings come from the Middle Ages, when women had both the opportunity and the interest to write about atonement. The abundance of writings by women in the medieval period is second only to that of our current day. While the status and opportunities for women were much more limited in the Middle Ages than they are today, those women who became nuns, beguines, recluses, and pilgrims had the time and resources to reflect on their Christian lives and record their reflections for posterity. Part of the impetus for this reflection was the sacramental context of the medieval church, which stressed the pilgrim status of Christians. Through baptism, followed by penance and good works, Christians built a life of virtue that realized the saving grace of God. In a post-Reformation age, this life is often denigrated as works righteousness, but it is better understood as a synergy of divine grace and human response. The current interest in medieval writings is due, in part, to the realization that our own age is striving for a similar balance of grace and faith.

Our study will begin with Julian of Norwich because her theology directly addresses the idea of atonement. An English recluse who lived in the age of the great plagues of Europe, Julian provides a basis for a paradigm shift in atonement theology. Her writing suggests a move away from Anselm's concern for satisfying the justice of God to a concern for the wellness of humanity. Building on the work of Joan Nuth, I argue that atonement is about the matter of satisfaction; however, that satisfaction is not something humanity needs to offer to God, but rather is a human need that God offers to us in Christ. Atonement theology begins in the subjective reality of our search for salvation and moves to the objective reality of God's love and grace. Its primary concern is to articulate salvation as a process of transformation that begins with personal healing and leads to social justice.

Building on insights from Julian's ideas about the nature of God's saving love, chapter 3 will discuss the experience of that love as described in the writings of Mechthild of Magdeburg. A beguine trained in the poetry of courtly love, Mechthild writes about the longing and ecstasy of loving God. Rather than the life-denying formula that sin plus love plus sacrifice equals salvation, Mechthild suggests that freedom plus love plus will for the other equals satisfaction. Such a description will clarify how the satisfying love of God saves us.

Completing this discussion of atonement, Hildegard of Bingen will provide a basis for thinking about the appropriate role of responding to the satisfying love of God. Her theology suggests a retrieval of the place of work—or, as she calls it, virtue—in the Christian life. Hildegard reminds us that not only are we saved from self-sacrifice, but we are saved for the satisfying work of creation. She provides a vision of salvation that equips us for the satisfying work of God.

Having outlined a new understanding of atonement as satisfying love, in Part 2 we will explore some of the ways one might live a satisfied life. Again, medieval mystics provide insightful reflection on some common and yet problematic themes of the Christian life. Margery Kempe, who had at least one interview with Julian of Norwich, attempted to live a satisfied life through a process of pilgrimage. She traveled all over the known world in search of satisfaction, and her poignant autobiography shows a real-life example of the difficulty of living a satisfied life. It is not a perfect example of satisfaction, but instead inspires us with the passion and urgency of its quest.

Chapter 6 will turn to Hadewijch of Brabant for a discussion of service. An area of great reward and terrible exploitation for women, service is a reality that needs to be carefully rethought in a theology of atonement. Here Hadewijch serves as an example and sage, for she both lived the life of service as a beguine, and counseled others about the joys and dangers of the serving life. Her frank reappraisal of work as both noble service and suffering exile provides a basis for a contemporary understanding of Christian service.

Finally, Catherine of Siena will serve as the guide for reinterpretation of the meaning of suffering in the Christian life. No book on atonement would be complete without a discussion of suffering. Catherine of Siena, who lived a glorious and painful life of willing suffering, confronts us with the reality of Christian suffering. Can a contemporary theology affirm the reality and power of Catherine's suffering (indeed, all Christian suffering) without reinforcing the harmful notion that suffering satisfies God? This question returns us once again to the core of the Christian gospel, the crucifixion, and its place in a feminist theology of satisfying love.

Surrounded by the insights of Julian, Mechthild, Hildegard, Margery, Hadewijch, and Catherine, we will see that we are saved by the satisfying love of God, which calls us from a state of abusive self-sacrifice, for a life of searching, service, and even suffering in loving relation with God and God's creation. It is a satisfied life.

✱ ✱ ✱

PART ONE

SATISFACTION IN CHRISTIAN LIFE

chapter two

JULIAN OF NORWICH ON
BEING SATISFIED

J ulian of Norwich is a well-known figure to many contemporary
Christians. Living in England in the fourteenth century, she wrote
a book entitled *Revelations of Divine Love* that has captured the
imagination of many contemporary readers for its ideas about God's
love. Scholarly interest in her work often centers on the idea of
Christ as our mother, which correlates with contemporary interest
in feminine images of God. Beneath this description of God is an
understanding of the experience of saving love that provides new insight for
the question of salvation. Following the lead of recent studies by Grace
Jantzen and Denise Baker, this chapter will explore how Julian can be a guide
for a contemporary theology of atonement.

First, it is important to realize that the life Julian lived was anything but
contemporary. Enclosed in a chapel next to a church in Norwich, England,
Julian spent much of her adult life in solitary prayer and contemplation.
Such Christians, called anchoresses, were sanctioned by the church to live a
life of prayer for the benefit of the Christian world. In addition to praying,
Julian counseled fellow Christians. While she tells us nothing of these
encounters, they must have involved discussion of the massive suffering of
her day caused by the Hundred Years' War and the Black Death. In her own
town she would have witnessed the suffering caused by peasant uprisings and
the burning of the Lollards, a religious group known for their criticism of the
church.

Given these circumstances, one might understand the attraction of the enclosed life with its safety and relative security. To live such a life was not considered an escape from the world, but rather a unique calling to a life of contemplation for the world. Julian's calling came as a result of a near-death experience at the age of thirty. Having received the last rites of the church, she was told to focus her gaze on the cross, when she suddenly revived and experienced sixteen visions that centered on Christ's suffering. The event astounded her, and she puzzled over its meaning for at least twenty years. Like Roberta Bondi's dream, Julian's visions were a wake-up call about the meaning of salvation in the face of the massive suffering of her day. After this experience, she became an anchoress to contemplate the meaning of the cross. When she had worked through the theological implications of her experience, Julian wrote a book that recorded the revelations of divine love.

Joan Nuth has argued that Julian's insights are so exceptional that they deserve a place alongside the dominant theology of Anselm as a medieval model of atonement.[1] This, in part, is a claim that the mystical style of Julian's writing is every bit as theological as the scholastic theology of Anselm. She wrote for the "even-Christian," one who was familiar with spiritual writing but not literate in Latin. Anselm wrote for a scholastic audience, whose members spoke the language of theology. Julian's concern, like Roberta Bondi's concern, was the articulation of a theology that made sense of the experience of crucifixion.

Also like Bondi, Julian wanted to be in dialogue with the tradition of the church. That is why she provided a careful exegesis of her experience and in all ways gave reference to the authority of the church in her writing. She urged that her near-death experience was not the point; rather it was the deepened love of God and theological insights gained from it. This emphasis allows us to concentrate not on the validity of visions as a form of religious experience but on the validity of her theological insights. They are insights that deepen rather than counter basic Christian faith. She has been called a "subtle-strategist"[2] because she knew the language of atonement theology and used that language in ways that offered new insights. In Julian we have a conversation partner who can show us the way to think through the critique of atonement theology and emerge with a theology that is truly atoning.

THE THEORY OF SATISFACTIONARY ATONEMENT

To understand the contribution Julian makes to atonement theology, we need to look at the background of the dominant atonement theory of her time,

Anselm's theory of satisfaction. Anselm gained prominence because he focused on the crucifixion as the means of salvation and based his conclusion on the social context of sin. This key point is seen in the following passage from Book 1, Chapter 24, of his major work, *Cur Deus Homo* (Why God Became Man), in which Anselm outlined the problem of the divine-human relation:

> Suppose someone, for example, assigns some task to his servant and directs him not to throw himself into a pit which he points out to him, and from which he simply cannot escape. Suppose that servant, having no regard for the command and the warning of his master, voluntarily throws himself into the pit that has been pointed out to him, so that he cannot perform the task assigned. Do you think this inability can in any way excuse him from not performing the assigned task?[3]

In looking at what this passage says about the problem of what we are saved from, we see that the obvious answer is "the pit," which reminds us of the biblical passage of the Fall. The human condition is to fall into a pit from which we cannot escape. But the key phrase is the description of how we got there in the first place. "Having no regard for the command and the warning of his master, [the servant] voluntarily throws himself into the pit." We need to be saved from a willful disobedience to our master. That is why it is obvious that the servant cannot be excused. His action is not just stupid; it is dishonorable. His fall makes it impossible for the servant to complete his appointed work, and thus the servant shows no regard for the will (and the superior power and wisdom) of his master. In an earlier passage Anselm writes, "A person who does not render God this honor due Him, takes from God what is His and dishonors God, and this is to commit sin."[4] In short, sin tarnishes the honor of God.

Why is this so crucial? We are created to do our assigned task, which is not only to do God's work, but to do so respectfully and honorably. Otherwise, we will have a world of chaos in which servants do not obey their master's commands. "The will of every rational creature," Anselm writes, "must be subject to the will of God."[5] Underneath this story is the assumption that salvation, as well as social order, comes from honoring God. In answer to the question of what we are saved for, Anselm argues that we are saved for giving honor to God.

Therefore, salvation requires restoring honor to God. We are saved by doing the work of God and, more important, by repaying respect to God. But it is difficult to imagine how one can pay for the defamation of God's character, because justice requires repayment plus compensation for damaging God's honor. Anselm calls this satisfaction. Of course, the disregarding servant is unable to do anything, since he cannot even get out of the pit, and so only Christ can do the work of obeying God plus paying back respect. The crucifixion—a noncompulsory death that pays back more to God than is owed—is the work that makes satisfaction and restores honor to God. We are saved by the satisfactionary work of Christ, which restores justice and order to the cosmos. Thus Anselm's theology is often called the satisfactionary model (or justice theory) of atonement.

There are a number of reasons why Anselm's theology, complete with the medieval notions of honor and justice, has resonated with Christians long beyond the medieval time of duty and order. For one thing, Anselm provided a necessary reason for the crucifixion of Christ. He showed the way for Christians to defend their faith against Jews and Muslims. Sin so destroyed the fabric of creation that neither following the Torah nor submitting to the will of Allah was enough to restore order. Only a savior whose voluntary death offered satisfaction would accomplish restoration. This idea also set atonement in the context of the lived faith of the church by helping worshipers make sense of the creeds, especially the Creed of Chalcedon's claim that Jesus was fully human as well as fully divine. Only one fully divine could make satisfaction; only one fully human ought to pay satisfaction. Thus it concurred with what Christians confessed at worship to be true faith. Thirdly, Anselm's theology is based in social reality. It sought to make sense of atonement as not only an interpersonal relationship between the Christian and God, but a social order that is centered in a just society. Thus it has had lasting value as a theology that attempts to make sense of the world as well as God.

The question is, therefore, does it make sense of the world as we know it? Liberation theologians have questioned the validity of Anselm's theory of satisfaction because it does not embody principles of justice. One concern is the social ethics implied in Anselm's theology. While Anselm suggests that paying satisfaction to God restores justice, liberation theologians argue that justice comes through solidarity with God, which heals the broken order of the universe. Furthermore, Anselm suggests that the means for healing the order of the universe is sacrificial death, which implies that the taking of human lives is theologically justified. Liberation theologians argue that the taking of human life, whether voluntary or not, is the basis of oppression, not of justice. A theology that justifies oppression offers a strange form of justice.[6]

And what about God? Does Anselm make sense of what Christians believe about God? Differences in atonement theories result from differences in understanding the divine-human relationship. Vincent Brümmer observes that the consequence of Anselm's theology is the idea that we value heaven more than we value God and God values honor more than God values us.[7] Satisfaction is a relationship that disregards the other as a means to an end. The real goals are heaven and honor rather than reconciliation. Another way to say this is that a restored order in which God is honored and we are saved is more important than the restoration of the relationship between the Christian and God. Many critics have argued that Anselm's theology conveys the idea of a wrathful or angry God, but this is really not the problem. Rather, the problem is this disregard of God and by God. The consequence of Anselm's concern to preserve the justice of God is a notion of God as too distant to be angry.[8]

Most troubling is the meaning and work of salvation conveyed in this understanding of the divine-human exchange. Anselm's notion has usually been characterized as articulating an objective theory of atonement, by which theologians mean it places emphasis on atonement as the work of God, not of human endeavor. A core premise is that humans cannot pay satisfaction; only God can. Thus salvation is divine work, and Christ must be fully divine. If we are looking for a theory that reinforces the truth that we do not save ourselves, Anselm seems to be the answer. But if we look more closely, we see that underneath the fact that humans cannot pay satisfaction is the premise that humans ought to satisfy God. Sin and salvation, according to Anselm, are properly human work. It is the servant's task to do the work assigned to him. Refusing to do this work harms not primarily humans, who should receive no pity for their willful fall, but God, whose honor is harmed.

This leads to a startling conclusion. Salvation is a divine need and the work of salvation is properly a human action. That is why Christ must be fully human to do saving work. Humans ought to pay satisfaction. Christ's act of atonement makes it possible for humans to return to a relationship that can repay God for sin. It is no wonder that as Anselm's theory gains dominance, the church becomes more and more wedded to a system of penance that cod-

ifies a multitude of ways in which humans can pay for sin to satisfy God.
Furthermore, in our day, we cling to the idea that paying satisfaction to whatever we have put in the place of God—our families, our work, our society, our
church—will save us. Like Roberta Bondi we may think that self-sacrificial
love can make everything all right.

THE THEOLOGY OF BEING SATISFIED
The key question is whether there is truth in the premise that humans ought
to make satisfaction for sin. Is this how we are saved? It is a question that
Julian of Norwich struggled with for more than twenty years. She lived three
hundred years after Anselm, and her visions (she called them showings) made
her question the meaning of satisfaction. While we have no way of knowing
whether she was a student of Anselm's theology, Julian does tell us that Christ
taught her to "contemplate the glorious atonement" (*SHL*, 29).[9] It is curious
that her deepest contemplation on this theme is based on the same hypo-
thetical situation of a servant in a pit that we saw above in Anselm's writing:

> I saw two persons in bodily likeness, that is to say a lord and a ser-
> vant; and with that God gave me spiritual understanding. The lord
> sits in state, in rest and in peace. The servant stands before his lord,
> respectfully, ready to do his lord's will. The lord looks on his servant
> very lovingly and sweetly and mildly. He sends him to a certain
> place to do his will. Not only does the servant go, but he dashes off
> and runs at great speed, loving to do his lord's will. And soon he
> falls into a dell and is greatly injured; and then he groans and moans
> and tosses about and writhes, but he cannot rise or help himself in
> any way. And of all this, the greatest hurt which I saw him in was
> lack of consolation, for he could not turn his face to look on his lov-
> ing lord. . . . Then this courteous lord said this: See my beloved ser-
> vant, what harm and injuries he has had and accepted in my service
> for my love, yes, and for his good will. Is it not reasonable that I
> should reward him for his fright and his fear, his hurt and his
> injuries and all his woe? And furthermore, is it not proper for me to
> give him a gift, better for him and more honourable than his own
> health could have been? Otherwise, it seems to me that I should be
> ungracious. (*SHL*, 51)

The first thing that is striking about this vision is the way the servant is depicted. He does not disregard God. His problem is not disobedience but lack of consolation. He remains full of good will and ready to do his lord's will (*SHL*, 51). The challenge of Julian is to question the reality that God imputes blame to the servant. Implicit in Anselm is the right, even the necessity, of God to blame us for fallenness. With Julian there is no cause for blame. She notes that she looked to see if the lord would impute blame to the servant and to her amazement "truly none was seen" (*SHL*, 51). At another point Julian writes that "between God and our soul there is neither wrath nor forgiveness in his sight" (*SHL*, 46). We do not need to be saved from willful disregard of God's will. This is why at another point Julian argues that sin is "no deed" (*SHL*, 11), implying that sin is not disobedience.

THE HUMAN NEED FOR SATISFACTION

What, then, is the problem? We still have a servant who has fallen in a dell and cannot get out. In fact Julian notes that she can see "no help for him" (*SHL*, 51). Amid his physical pains, she sees that his greatest problem is that he cannot see the compassionate reaction of his lord. So in his fallen condition, he can only dwell on his pain and distress until he is "blinded in his reason and perplexed in his mind, so much so that he had almost forgotten his own love" (*SHL*, 51). There is no lack of blame in this vision of sin. However, the placing of blame is a human reaction, not a divine one.

The problem is that blame is very real in human experience. It is an injury to human nature that is manifested in the physical separation of the lord and servant. Here sin is shown as physical suffering, and the effect of sin is the preoccupation with suffering. Julian outlines seven pains that are the result of the servant's fall; these seven pains mirror the traditional listing of seven deadly sins. Sin is certainly as real in Julian's theology as in Anselm's, but here sin is lamentable rather than contemptible. As Brant Pelphrey notes, sin is seen here as a sickness.[10] In another passage Julian writes, "Sin is the sharpest scourge with which any chosen soul can be struck, which scourge belabours man or woman, and breaks a man, and purges him in his own sight so much that at times he thinks himself that he is not fit for anything but as it were to sink into hell" (*SHL*, 39). To feel worthless, especially in the eyes of God, is the essence of sin. It is indeed dishonor, but of one's self, not of God.

The reason for this dishonor is the internalization of wrath that one mistakenly thinks comes from God. It is projection of self-wrath onto God. Julian writes, "For wrath is nothing else but a perversity and an opposition to peace and love. And it comes from a lack of power or a lack of wisdom or a lack of goodness, and this lack is not in God, but it is on our side" (*SHL*, 48). Here Julian builds on the reasonable assumption that a perfect God cannot be lacking in those absolute qualities of power, wisdom, or goodness. Her insight is seeing that wrath is not an absolute quality but the lack of perfect being, which is manifest in the imperfection of human existence. Seeing the servant as symbolic of the state of humanity, Julian concludes that the human condition is one of self-accusation. "For it is for man meekly to accuse himself " (*SHL*, 52).

In the dell, the servant does not have the power to turn his face; thus he cannot know how his lord has responded to his failed mission, and as a result he has lost all sense of his own intrinsic goodness. All he can do is meditate on his failure. Thus sin "subverts the focus of the gaze, from grace to works."[11] This misdirected focus on the imperfection of our human actions has the power to inflict suffering and separate humanity from God. Therefore, sin blinds us to the gaze of God. It is the inability of the servant to "look on his loving lord." "And so," Julian concludes, "in the servant there was shown the blindness and the hurt of Adam's falling" (*SHL*, 52). The fall is the blindness of the self to God's love.

Furthermore, Julian talks about "secret sins" that result from the blindness of self-blame. They are impatience and despair, which result from the fear of God's might and wisdom (*SHL*, 73). Knowing that God knows he has failed and that only God has the power to do anything about his predicament, the servant falls into despair. It is impatience that got him into this mess in the first place, and nothing he has experienced so far has changed this weakness in his character, but now it is coupled with despair that God's might will turn against him. Julian concludes that he ends up in a place that is narrow, comfortless, and distressful (*SHL*, 51). It is the pit of human dishonor.

THE GRACE OF DIVINE COURTESY

If we need to be saved from dishonor of self, salvation is the restoration of self. Julian sees that sin "will be turned into high, surpassing honor and endless bliss" (*SHL*, 51). Here honor is not something God needs; rather it is a human need. As Brad Peters notes, sin, as real as it is, is beside the point. The real task of the Christian is to recognize God's gaze (129). It is to understand the nature and action of God.

When the lord asks if it is not reasonable to reward the servant, we are shocked. At least nineteen of the twenty years of Julian's reflection must have concerned this point. To say that God honors us for our sin is to tear at the social order of our universe. It mocks Anselm's notion of justice and breaks down the hierarchy of master and servant. And this may be the point. A key to understanding the nature of God is to understand what Julian means when she describes God as a "courteous lord" (*SHL*, 51). The second original insight on Julian's part is to cast the divine-human relationship in terms of the idea of courtesy.

Julian talks about the courtesy of God more than thirty times. Today we trivialize courtesy as old-fashioned manners or proficiency in the performance of the arts of social grace. But in the medieval society of Julian's day, courtesy was revered as the highest form of relationship. It was associated with the world of courtly love, and its main characteristic was people treating one another with kindness. In a world of arranged marriages and feudal order, courtly love was the rare voluntary relationship of a lady and her lord made famous in the legend of Lancelot and Guinevere. As lovers of God, mystics of the Middle Ages used the idea of this rare relationship to talk about the experience of love of God. As applied to God, it denotes liberality, goodness, and grace.[12]

Without courtesy, Julian sees, the lord would seem ungracious. What is unusual is not the gracious reaction of the lord, but that he acts with courtesy toward a servant. In the medieval world of courtly love, courtesy was practiced only between members of the same class. This is why later in her remarks, Julian spends an inordinate amount of time talking about the nature of the servant's dress. He is dressed in a white tunic that is old, worn, tight-fitting, short, and ready to go to rags. Such dress should denote a person of lower status whose worth is reflected in his attire. But, she notes, his clothes are not fitting, for they do not match his heart. He is evidently of higher status than his looks indicate.

If a courteous relationship is based on the reciprocal love of persons of like status, then Julian is implying that the core of humanity must contain a likeness to God. Remember that the servant is not disobedient, but lovingly does the lord's will, and his injuries are a result of his desire for service. There is a social fabric to atonement, but it is not the order of a just world of master and servant. It is the saved world of courteous relation. As we noted before, God cannot be unkind or wrathful, because unkindness comes from a lack of power, wisdom, and goodness. Similarly, God does not blame the servant for the fall but desires to reward him because his actions are the result of goodwill. Sin—the dishonoring of self—is a denial of the truth of our being. "Here we see," Julian writes, "that truly it belongs to our nature to hate sin, and truly it belongs to us by grace to hate sin, for nature is all good and fair in itself, and grace was sent out to save nature and destroy sin, and bring fair nature back again to the blessed place from which it came, which is God, with more nobility and honour by the powerful operation of grace" (*SHL*, 63). To experience salvation is to realize the full potential of being created in the image and likeness of God.

The reward of salvation is to grow into the fullness of our humanity. Julian calls this "oneing," and it is the process of growing into one-ness with God. Just as love grows when we realize that our worth in another's eyes is not based on what we do for the other, but who we are, so Julian is able to say that the servant will be rewarded above what he would have been had he not fallen. Like most mystics who talk about union with God based on love, Julian imagines a "oneing" that is not a dissolving of self, but a meeting of the soul in God. Her phrase for this is "knitting" to God (*SHL*, 53), and Andrew Sprung notes that by this Julian means a weaving of one's soul to God.[13]

Talk of reward also leads Julian to some interesting speculation about the possibility of universal salvation. If our natural condition is goodwill, and sin is a human problem, not divine, then is it not logical that all are saved? Here Julian is trying to think through what it means to eliminate mistrust in the forgiveness of God. One result is her popular phrase "all things shall be well," which is an eschatological statement that in the goodness of God, "all things must, inevitably, come to good."[14] That is the hope of all Christians. Whether or not it applies to those who do not see themselves in relation to Christianity is another point. She even contemplates the possibility that Jews are not condemned, which was heresy in her day. Finally, she has to conclude that she cannot see their condemnation, although she knows it must be true because the church teaches it (*SHL*, 33). Here Julian comes to the end of the logic of the vision of the lord and servant. While we might like to applaud her pluralistic spirit, it is important to remember that her main concern is not to understand if Jews are worthy of God's love, but to further contemplate the grace of realizing she is worthy of the courtesy of God.

THE SAVING WORK OF DIVINE SATISFACTION

But realizing one's worth is not an easy matter. How will the servant receive the word that his lord intends to reward him? Who will turn his face to God? Here again, Julian turns the theology of satisfactionary atonement on its head. While wrath is a human response, not divine, and honor is a human need, not God's, likewise, satisfaction is a divine action, not a human one. The necessary reason for the mission of Christ is not human sin, but human satisfaction.[15] In order to be saved, we need Christ to come tell us that we are loved in the sight of God. In an amazing conversation between herself and Christ, Julian realizes the true meaning of satisfaction. "Then our good Lord put a question to me: Are you well satisfied that I suffered for you? I said: Yes, good Lord, all my thanks to you; yes, good Lord, blessed may you be. Then Jesus our good Lord said: If you are satisfied, I am satisfied" (SHL, 22). We are not saved by satisfying God's honor, but by being satisfied that God loves us.

What an amazing conversation. Imagine Jesus asking you if you are satisfied! No wonder Julian stumbles around in her answer. It is not a conversation of a servant looking up from a ditch but of servant and servant side by side in courteous relation. For as Julian looks at her vision of the lord and servant she realizes that the servant not only represents us, but also represents Christ, who comes into our midst to give us a new perspective on our intrinsic worth.

Here Christ's work is primarily one of bringing the message to the servant in the dell that God will reward him for his goodwill, not punish him for his failure. It is the important work of helping the servant see through God's eyes, not his own. It is based on the realization that God's vision is not ours. God sees with the double vision of compassion for Adam and rejoicing for Christ. The servant, a representative of Adam, has limited spatial vision and cannot see the loving gaze of God outside the dell. But Christ brings to the servant news of God's limitless vision of compassion. Secondly, Christ comes to communicate the eternal time frame of God's vision. The servant knows only the present, when he has failed to do God's work. God sees not only the present failure of the servant (Adam) but the good work of the servant (Christ). In the eternal framework of God, past and present are wrapped in the future when all will be well. "When God sees us, even in our sin, God sees Christ."[16]

THE SATISFACTION OF DIVINE SUFFERING

Julian is suggesting an existential understanding of atonement in which the Fall and the incarnation are coterminous events. Atonement is not interested in progress, a type of saving work, but in being, a saving relationship. So when Julian turns to describing how Jesus shows us God's love, she does not dwell on the death of Christ as atoning work, but on the incarnation of Christ as atoning relationship. Christ is characterized as the gardener, an image that comes from John 20, where Mary encounters the risen Christ at the tomb and mistakes him for a gardener.[17] As gardener, Christ is sent to uncover treasure in the earth that God loves. The treasure is humanity, and the process of uncovering this treasure is hard work. It involves digging and ditching and sweating and turning the soil over, and watering the plants (SHL, 51). Like any good relationship, it takes a lifetime of caring for and cultivating the relationship in order to grow into courteous love. It is the work of Christ drawing us into union with God.

The suffering of Christ is part of this cultivation. It is certainly true that Julian is concerned with making sense of the suffering of Christ. Her visions are filled with reflection, often graphic and gory, on the crucifixion. In her discussion of satisfaction she describes the suffering of Christ as a "noble, precious and honourable deed, performed once in time by the operation of love" (SHL, 22). By going beyond the normal work of creation, the crucifixion reveals the limitless nature of the courtesy God extends to humanity. Such work demonstrates the high respect of God for us and leads Julian to the amazing truth that we are God's honor, God's crown. The sin of unworthiness is overcome and honor is restored to us. "And this," she writes, "was a singular wonder and a most delectable contemplation" (SHL, 22).

Suffering, therefore, is properly the action of God and God alone. To imitate Christ's suffering would be to assume that God needs to be convinced of our respect, a notion that is inconsistent with the eternal and limitless vision of God. Thus Julian is forced to realize that her earlier desire to suffer with Christ was based on a false understanding of the nature of God. Julian's mature contemplation of the passion of Christ is meant to evoke the reality of God's love for us, not the model of our love for God. I agree here with David Aers, who notes that Julian's images of the suffering of Jesus are always seen as part of the Trinity, so that we understand that Christ's passion is divine action rather than a model for redemptive suffering.[18]

This may be why immediately following her vision of the lord and servant, Julian begins talking about Christ as our mother (SHL, 60–61), who labors us into birth through the blood, pain, and suffering on the cross. Furthermore, Christ feeds us through communion; thus highlighting God's saving action as present experience as well as past event. Motherhood, Julian argues, is the best model we have for the nature of an unconditional and limitless love. It best describes Christ's stunning confession that if he could have suffered more for us, he would (*SHL*, 60). The point here is to remind Christians that in relation to God we are children, not mothers. "The precious love of motherhood has made him [Jesus] our debtor" (*SHL*, 60). Like the relation of master to servant, in the realm of God, even the relation of mother to child becomes a courteous relation.

THE CONTRITE LIFE OF SATISFACTION

So what is the response of the Christian to the motherly love of God? Julian notes two things. First, we are to trust in the motherly love of God in "wellbeing and woe." Julian likens the role of God to the role of a good mother who disciplines us as children and knows when to stand by and let us learn from our own mistakes. As we grow, God responds to our needs, guarding us in our infancy and chastising us in our youth so that we will grow in virtue and grace. Throughout her work, Julian sees God's love, which requires only that we trust in and return that love (*SHL*, 61). While that love will not eliminate the suffering in our lives, whether imposed by outside forces or internal failure, Julian urges us not to dwell on it. Instead, we are to dwell on the constant love of God. Therefore, it is the servant's responsibility to trust in God's benevolence, even when he is in the dell.

Since it is impossible for the servant to see beyond his own suffering, Julian notes that his second responsibility is to commit himself "fervently to the faith of Holy Church" (*SHL*, 61) because even when one person is broken, the entire body of the church is never all broken. Thus, in times of woe one can be fed by the well-being of fellow Christians. Furthermore, all are fed by communion, which is like mother's milk, nourishing us in the love of God. Through partaking of the body of our Mother Christ in the community of Mother Church, we can catch a glimpse of the timeless love of God.

Beyond this admonition to stay in the church, Julian does not give us much guidance in how to develop trust in God's love. Yet plenty of people attend a church service every Sunday and have yet to develop such trust. Julian's writing does not dwell on the progress or stages of the Christian life. We will be caught in the woe of sin, she notes, "until contrition seizes [us] by the inspiration of the Holy Spirit and turns bitterness into hope of God's mercy. And then the wounds begin to heal and the soul to revive, restored to the life of Holy Church" (SHL, 39). Contrition is the wearing away of something hard, here understood as the wearing away of self-blame and the feeling of dishonor. It will involve the reorientation of the human toward God, which will come as the result of God's special grace in our lives and the continuing grace found in the community of faith.

Since little is known about Julian, it is impossible to know exactly how this process worked in her life. However, a comparison of her final edition of *Revelations of Divine Love* with an earlier edition that was written soon after her illness (often referred to as the "Short Text") gives evidence that she is speaking from her own experience of having her self-image healed and her soul revived. She hints at this process when she notes that understanding of the meaning of the parable of the lord and servant was not given to her at the time of the revelations (SHL, 51). In fact, all discussion of the parable as well as of Jesus as mother is included only in her later writing.

Julian gives us a glimpse of her growing sense of self in a chapter about her role as teacher. In her earlier writing, she asks the reader to "disregard the wretched worm, the sinful creature to whom it was shown" (SHS, 6). She follows this with the admonition, "God forbid that you should say or assume that I am a teacher, for that is not and never was my intention; for I am a woman, ignorant, weak and frail" (SHS, 6). Whether these remarks reflect her sense of self or are written to make her more acceptable to her readers is hard to say. What is striking is that her later edition omits this entire passage and replaces it with the simple statement that "everything that I say about me I mean to apply to all my fellow Christians, for I am taught that this is what our Lord intends in this spiritual revelation" (SHL, 8). Such a statement displays a remarkable sense of self-worth that is completely lacking in the earlier version.

Two other passages support this conclusion. In pondering the necessity of sin, she first notes that she lacked discretion and was filled with pride. Yet in the latter version she recalls this same event but eliminates the phrase "filled with pride," seeming to realize that in her earlier days being filled with pride was the least of her problems (SHS, 13; SHL, 27). Another clue comes near the end of her account when Julian describes how she originally doubted the authenticity of her experience, exclaiming, "See what a wretched creature I am!"(SHS, 21). In the later edition she writes, "See how wretched I was!" (SHL, 66). Together, Julian gives us the impression of a contrite and satisfied soul.

CONTEMPORARY REFLECTIONS

In Julian's theology we have a rich resource for constructing a contemporary understanding of atonement. To do so is to realize that contemporary feminist concerns about atonement theology are not unique but rest in a history of Christian reflection on the meaning of satisfaction in the lives of Christian women. Feminist theology did not invent the question of whether self-sacrifice and self-negation are the solution or the problem of the Christian life. Neither is it unique in criticizing Anselm's understanding of satisfaction as the meaning of salvation.

What we need to build on is Julian's insight that satisfaction is not about restoring honor to God but about the human need to be assured of God's love. This perspective provides a paradigm shift in atonement theology. One of the strengths of this model is that it properly sees the objective reality of atonement as the satisfying action of God. A theology of atonement should start with the humble confession that it is a human need to be atoned. We are the ones with the problem and the problem is judging our worth according to our limited vision of reality. Underneath the sacrificial acts of Christians, one often finds a sense of unworthiness. Failure to earn the love of others is turned inward to a sense of being unworthy of love. Central to feminist theology is the realization that sin is not always willful disobedience manifested as pride. More often, sin is the negation of self. The need, as Janet Schaller notes, is not the emptying of self but the emptying of negation of the self.[19] It is the need to begin with the conviction that we are created in the image and likeness of God.

Therefore, Julian helps us articulate how the problem of sin results from a misunderstanding of the nature of ourselves and of God. A central insight of this view of atonement is that wrath is not a divine characteristic but a human projection of unworthiness onto God. Julian is right when she argues that it is logically inconsistent to think of atonement as satisfying the wrath of God. Wrath, she notes, is about lack of power, wisdom, and goodness. God, properly understood, is powerful, wise, and good. These qualities merge into an eternal vision that sees not only the present condition of human sin, but the future condition of Christ's victory over sin. The idea that we must appease the wrath of God is the problem of, not the solution to, sin.

With this spatial rather than linear perspective, Julian's theology has a modern ring. Anselm's theology of atonement is built on the Augustinian notion of the historical nature of salvation. The creation and fall of Adam are historical events in which humanity receives and then loses its essential goodness. But in modern theology these events are understood in an existential rather than historical framework. Thus the creation and fall of Adam describe the ambiguity of our God-given and yet fallen identity. Likewise, Julian realizes that atonement theology needs to see the creation, fall, and redemption of humanity as aspects of the relationship with God, not sequential events. To see with the eyes of God is to understand that God sees our lives in the framework of Christ's saving work. Atonement is not primarily about the event of past salvation, but the experience of being saved.

Such an understanding rests on a reconception of the divine-human relationship as a courteous relation. The master-servant relationship central to Anselm's theology is reimagined as a relationship of loving friends. God loves us because we are created in the image of God and that image is made manifest to us in the work of Christ. We are not God, but we have the potential to be the friends of God. Atonement is about realizing that friendship, trusting in it, and feeding on it. Feminists have rightfully criticized theological conceptions that portray God as an omnipotent power over creation. Power works in and through relationships as God works in and through us and all of creation. The depth of that power is seen in the courtesy of the incarnation, which shows God's respect, affirmation, and love. The crucifixion is the ultimate expression of that power, which in its limitless courtesy satisfies us of the loyalty and love of God.

Here we must be careful not to build on Julian's idea of divine motherhood as a model for Christian life. While it is true that Julian sees giving birth and breast-feeding as ways of describing the meaning of the work of Christ in crucifixion and communion, she stresses that to God we are not mothers. Christ asks Julian if she is satisfied, not if she satisfies. Julian does not suggest an equality between us and God. We are friends with, but not equals to, God. Our vision is limited, but God's vision is limitless both in terms of time and space. Thus the idea of God as our mother has some potential for underscoring that satisfaction is not human work and that we are saved from satisfying God. But the idea of humanity as helpless children does not adequately describe the human condition or help us address the dilemma of how we are saved.

The problem is that we are not innocent children who are victims of a sinful world that promotes self-sacrifice. We are free and willing agents who not only fail to see, but also intentionally ignore, the love of God. The goodwill of the servant does not describe wholly the complexity of our relationship with God. Here the idea of friendship may be a better model for the divine-human relationship than that between mother and child because the former suggests an ability on the part of both parties to accept or reject the offer of relationship. It is necessary to balance Julian's insights about the underlying cause of sin with the traditional understanding that sin manifests itself in a self-imposed bondage of the will. Julian helps us see that the roots of this bondage are impatience, despair, and ultimately fear of unworthiness, but she gives us little insight into the reality that it is self-imposed.

Therefore, it is hard to conceptualize how sin is overcome in the Christian life. Julian's idea of contrition gives us the vocabulary to think about salvation as the wearing away of worthlessness, but makes it hard to grasp how this is experienced in the life of faith. The image of Christ as gardener gives us vocabulary to imagine how this entails a process of growth and cultivation of love. The idea that contrition begins when we are seized by the Holy Spirit suggests that divine initiative is a necessary precondition for growth. The image of Christ as our mother who nourishes us in communion suggests the ongoing means of our cultivation. But Julian stops short of helping us see how we can participate in or respond to this saving work. If we are indeed in courteous relation with God, we must understand the nature of our courteous response.

Likewise, Julian gives us little insight into the purpose of salvation. Returning to the critique of Anselm, we need to answer the question of whether or not a feminist theology grounded in the theology of Julian makes sense of the world. Does Julian's idea of sin as self-blame address the violence in our world and provide a solution for social injustice? Here we can affirm that Julian intentionally focuses on the divine-human relationship rather than just social relations. While I have argued that the traditional division of objective and subjective theories of atonement is misleading, it is true that Julian focuses on the Christian as the subject of salvation. Given the contemporary context, in which we mistakenly think that salvation comes through our works, this is a good place to begin. In addition, Julian can help us see how the roots of suffering and violence are found in the rejection of the goodness of our creation in the image of God. It can help us get at the cause of violence and can show that the social disorder of our day is healed through addressing the psychological roots of violence. But it does not give a vision of how the work of God in Christ reconciles the world.

A theology of atonement that responds to the social injustice of our world begins with the realization that atonement is about the process of being satisfied that God loves us. This theology will celebrate with Julian the honorable action of God's satisfying love, and we will remember that we are saved from, not for, sacrifice. But such a theology does not fully understand the process and purpose of becoming satisfied. For that, we will need to turn to the writing of two other medieval mystics, Mechthild of Magdeburg and Hildegard of Bingen. First, we need to explore more fully the nature of the divine-human relationship as a courteous relation. Then we need to turn to the way in which this heavenly relationship reshapes our earthly relations. But the insight of Julian of Norwich has laid the groundwork for a feminist theology of atonement that can satisfy our desire to make sense of the gospel message that we do not save ourselves.

✳ ✳ ✳

MECHTHILD OF MAGDEBURG ON
SATISFYING LOVE

This study has begun with Julian of Norwich, who opens up the concept of atonement with the fascinating revelation that atonement is not about satisfying God's justice, but being satisfied that God loves us. This is a truly refreshing approach that recenters theology as addressing our problem, which is dissatisfaction, and its source, which is an insecurity that we are unloved and unlovable.

However, Julian does not provide insight into the experience of that saving love. For an understanding of the process of being satisfied, we will turn to the writing of Mechthild of Magdeburg. While Julian reminds us that love is the answer, Mechthild is the one who lived it. It is Mechthild who writes about the transformative experience of being satisfied by God's love. And in her writing we find an amazing story of the love and longing for God that I will argue has some important lessons for what it means to construct a contemporary Christian theology that truly saves lives.

Mechthild of Magdeburg lived in the thirteenth century, during the zenith of a group of mystics called beguines. They were women who lived lives of service in devotion to God but were neither wives nor nuns. They have a contemporary appeal because they lived on the fringes of the church and yet grounded their lives in a devout sense of love of God, much in the same way that many of the most spiritual people of our day are associated tangentially, if at all, with the institutional church. Yet it was not long before the church of Mechthild's day became nervous about the freedom of the beguines. In 1261 the Synod of Magdeburg instructed beguines to obey parish priests. After struggles with church authority, Mechthild finally decided to retire to the convent at Helfta, where she wrote her final work amidst a community of women scholar-nuns.

Elizabeth Petroff has called Mechthild the literary ideal of the beguines' effort to be in the world but not of it.[1] Mechthild's writing is grounded in the age-old theme of love mysticism, which imagines the divine-human relationship as a partnership of lovers. While a bit shocking to us, this idea of thinking of God as our lover is as old as the Song of Songs. For women like Mechthild, who were married neither to a man nor the church, Christ became the ideal spouse and object of their devotion. But Mechthild adds to this tradition evocative language framed in the genre of courtly love. The soul becomes the Queen at court, Lady Love is her attendant, Christ is her Lord, and the experience of God is described as a series of exciting rendezvous.

It is definitely not reading for the faint of heart. While her work, entitled *The Flowing Light of the Godhead,* is divided into seven books, there is no order to the books or the work as a whole. At one point Mechthild does note how her relationship to God has changed through her life from being the playmate of God in her childhood, to a bride in her youth, and a housewife in her old age (7.3),[2] but these are stages of life more than progressions of love. While the temptation is to map out the linear development of love of God, this is not the point. The style flows back and forth from poetry to prose. One scholar argues that it is this flowing theme that unifies her work. It conveys not only her literary style but the content of the flowing nature of love.[3]

Mechthild's work may best be categorized as a "love note" that is meant to assure other spiritual people of the reality of God's love and the ups and downs of establishing a loving relationship.[4] Like many women, Mechthild was commanded to write about her spiritual experiences by her confessor (4.2). She used the familiar religious and secular imagery of her day to convey the depths of her relationship with God. We know her work was read by her contemporaries because at one point she responds to criticisms of one of her visions (see 6.36). The majority of her readers were probably fellow beguines, untrained in the scholastic language of theology, but well schooled in the popular language of love. Mechthild's writing would have inspired their own love of God.

What comes through in her work is the complexity of love of God. She shows us the passion and suffering of loving God. It is a full-grown love, a full-bodied love. Mechthild herself notes that love flows "first and foremost, with great tenderness; then with sublime intimacy; and now, with intense suffering" (6.20). In its tenderness is the reciprocal, vulnerable, and equal nature of love of God. Sublime intimacy brings a realization of the demands of love, the longing of love, and the confrontation with free will. Intense suffering reveals the estrangement and exile of love. It is as we further explore the depths of this tenderness, sublime intimacy, and intense suffering that we realize the flowing nature of God's love.

THE TENDERNESS OF LOVE

The tenderness of God's love is the theme of a much-repeated passage from the first book of *The Flowing Light of the Godhead*:

A fish in water does not drown.
A bird in the air does not plummet.
Gold in fire does not perish.
Rather, it gets its purity and its radiant color there.
God has created all creatures to live according to their nature.
How, then, am I to resist my nature?
I must go from all things to God,
Who is my Father by nature,
My Brother by his humanity,
My Bridegroom by love,
And I his bride from all eternity.
Don't you believe I feel him intensely?
He can both burn powerfully and cool consolingly.
Now do not be overly sad.

Then the bride of all delights goes to the Fairest of lovers in the secret chamber of the invisible Godhead. There she finds the bed and the abode of love prepared by God in a manner beyond what is human.

Lord, now I am a naked soul
And you in yourself are a well-adorned God.
Our shared lot is eternal life
Without death.

Then a blessed stillness
That both desire comes over them.
He surrenders himself to her,
And she surrenders herself to him.
What happens to her then—she knows—
And that is fine with me.
But this cannot last long.
When two lovers meet secretly,
They must often part from one another inseparably. (1.44)

The most prominent feature of this passage is the reciprocity of love. Even though descriptions of union with God are common in mystical writing, the mutuality of love that Mechthild describes is not the norm. In a union of blessed stillness there is an equal sharing that both desire. It is a "shared lot of eternal life." God gives Godself to the soul and she to God. It is a love of mutual need and mutual desire.

To suggest that God needs the soul recasts the power of God as the power of love. While Mechthild maintains traditional imagery in that as lovers, God is cast in the role of the husband and the soul as the wife, she understands this as a relationship of mutual power and vulnerability. "He surrenders himself to her, and she surrenders herself to him." At one point she records God as saying, "The abundance of my riches is yours alone. And even over me shall you hold sway. You are very dear to my heart" (2.25). This loving inclination that makes God vulnerable to the soul in return empowers Mechthild to show love and concern for God. Drawing on the biblical passage of the woman who anoints Jesus' head with oil (Mark 14:3–9), Mechthild even suggests that the soul can heal God. Noting that God is wounded for love of her soul, Mechthild asks to be able to anoint God and declares, "Lord, if you were to take me home with you, I would be your physician forever" (3.2). The strength of her love comes from an understanding of power that flows through Mechthild rather than over her. It is a fiery love that grows stronger through mutual affection. "The more ardent she remains, the sooner she bursts into flame. The more she burns, the more beautifully she glows. The more God's praise is spread abroad, the greater her desire becomes" (1.22).

To be in such a relationship with God involves great risk, because one can be consumed by love, especially a love as powerful as God's. Love can burn powerfully, and it is this characterization of God's love that is commonly imagined in Christian tradition. The love of God is like a burning bush that is too bright for Moses' human eyes. Yet Mechthild argues that love can also cool consolingly. A fish in water does not drown; she will not drown in God's presence. This is so because there is an equality between the soul and God. "Lady soul you are so utterly formed to my nature," says God, "that not the slightest thing can be between you and me" (1.44).

In one exchange, Mechthild considers the idea that God and the soul are two gold pennies of equal value and equal good. Yet she protests, wondering how her "wretchedness" can equal divine goodness. God replies that through goodwill and holy desire one can "make good whatever you want" (7.6). They are equal because they are of the same nature, both longing for the other, both working to grow in love with the other. Like all good relationships, through intensity, perseverance, and work the soul strives to bridge the gap that separates it from God.

Like Julian of Norwich, Mechthild has an understanding of the love of God that is grounded in an original interpretation of the Fall of humanity. Humanity is created in love so that God will have someone to love. "I shall make a Bride for myself," God declares, "who shall greet me with her mouth and wound me with her beauty. Only then does love really begin" (3.9). Adam and Eve are created after the pattern of the Son of God with true knowledge, holy senses, and free will so that they might be the brides of God. But their purity is poisoned through the fruit of the wrong tree and thus they lose the essential qualities needed to be God's lovers. In keeping with the ideas of courtly love, which assume that only those of equal rank can be lovers, Mechthild surmises that only a pure soul can be worthy of being the bride of God. After the Fall, the soul is deformed and too impure to be a lover of God. "Who might accept this filth?" God cries (3.9). In distress and suffering God grieves the loss of true love.

At another point Mechthild suggests that God turns to Mary (who is not poisoned by sin) as a bride so as to have someone to love since the soul is dead to God. Mary provides needed companionship to God and fills the void of loss in God. She becomes the mother of the Son of God and the beloved of the Holy Spirit. Mary then nurtures those who long to return to God, beginning with the prophets, then Jesus, and then the apostles (1.22). But the work of reconciliation between humanity and God is accomplished by Christ, who restores humanity to its original relationship with God. The Son of God accomplishes this reconciliation by healing the wounds of humanity and atoning for human sin in his death (3.9). Mary continues to nurture the faithful with her protection, chastity, constancy, kindness, and patient hope (1.22).

Amy Hollywood notes that the point of this salvation history is to show God's faithfulness in love.[5] Grace is necessary because of the poisoning of the human soul in sin, but the original intention is for the soul to be of the same nature as God so that the soul may love God. Christ reclaims this nature for humanity, and through reclaiming our free will to love, we can indeed reclaim our lover, God. Like Julian, Caroline Bynum suggests that Mechthild reconciles the sin and sinlessness of humanity by suggesting we have two natures, one sinful, the other sinless.[6] However, Mechthild adds the idea that our sinless nature lies in Mary, who did not sin and became the bride of God when humanity fell. Because we are nurtured by Mary, who is our model for love, and healed by Christ, who enables our ability to love and be loved, we too can reenter a loving relationship with God.

THE SUBLIMENESS OF LOVE

This understanding of the sinless yet fragile nature of humanity leads Mechthild to a further understanding of the possibilities and limitations of love. For in understanding, she begins to realize the freedom that is inherent in the nature of love:

> I shall fall terribly sick from this,
> For I am bound to you.
> The bond is stronger than I am,
> Thus I cannot become free of love.
> I cry out to you in great longing,
> A lonely voice;
> I hope for your coming with heavy heart,
> I cannot rest, I am on fire,
> Unquenchable in your burning love.
> I pursue you with all my might.
> If I had the strength of a giant
> And if I got onto your trail,
> Still I would quickly lose your tracks.
> Please, my Love, run not so far ahead of me

And tarry a while in love,
So that I can catch you.
. . . [And God answers]
Your secret sighs shall reach me.
Your heart's anguish can compel me.
Your sweet pursuit shall so exhaust me
That I shall yearn to cool myself
In your limpid soul,
To which I have been bound.
The sighs and tremors of your wounded heart
Have driven out my justice from you.
That suits you quite well, as it does me:
I cannot be without you.
No matter how far we are apart,
We can still never be really separated.
No matter how softly I caress you,
I inflict immense pain on your poor body.
If I were to surrender myself to you continuously, as you desire,
I would lose my delightful dwelling place on earth within you. (2.25)

Here we begin to see the pain and longing of love of God. Mechthild is painfully aware of the limitations of earthly existence and her inability to control God's love. As she struggles to remain in the world, she must endure the absence of God. Longing is a common theme in courtly love poetry, and Mechthild uses it to describe the anxious waiting and lack of control over her lover's comings and goings. What is intriguing is the longing of God conveyed in this passage as well. God is wearied by Mechthild's pursuit and knows that the kind of presence she longs for is not humanly possible. However lightly God touches her, the effect is immense pain. And so a delicate dance of longing begins. Mechthild must come to understand the meaning of free will in the relationship of love. For whatever it means, it is beyond justice and she must trust that this will suit them both well.

This understanding of freedom forces Mechthild to confront her own desire for self-control as she comes to realize that self-will can interrupt the flowing of God's love. At one point she records Christ's lament: "People drive me from the shelter of their heart with their selfishness," Christ declares, "and when I find no room in them, I let them be in their selfishness" (7.13).

She confesses that even she is guilty of this obstinacy, which creates a mountain of darkness and distance between herself and God (4.5). In Book 7, Mechthild writes, "Alas, wretched brood, as long as we storm around in anger, even if there is anything good about us, we still have to come back to our heart. Then we must rightly be ashamed. The anger consumed our strength and dried out our flesh, and so we wasted our valuable time when we should have been serving God. Alas, this is an eternal loss! Again, alas! I regret the sinful tears that were shed in haughty anger" (7.3).

Mechthild must come face to face with her own limitation that she cannot summon her lover at her command. At first she focuses her anger on her body, calling it her enemy (4.2) because it impedes her ability to keep up with God. If only she had the strength of giants, she laments, then she could catch up with God. But as it is, her body cannot be touched without causing immense pain. Thus she admits that for twenty years she tried to conquer her body in an effort to summon God's love. But in a moment of revelation God urges her to follow and trust God in all things, saying, "everything that you need for body and soul I shall give you" (4.2). From this experience she comes to a new understanding that her limitation is not her physical nature but her lack of trust in the promise of her lover that "no matter how far we are apart, we can still never be really separated." So profound is this insight that her confessor orders her to write down her experiences and it is then that she undertakes the difficult task of trying to write "out of God's heart and mouth" (4.2).

In her writings, Mechthild suggests that the distance from God is not the result of the natural limitation of her body but the spiritual limitations placed on love by self-will. This will to control another she identifies as false holiness, which is named as the true nature of sin. Mechthild envisions three kinds of people, identified as children in distress, who exemplify false holiness and its possible cure. The first child refuses to use its free will to love God and remains distant from God by its own selfish will. The third child turns away from God's love because of its self-willed struggle with truth so that it judges wrongly all that it sees and hears. As a result it falls into contentiousness, false consolation, despair, and finally falls away from God's grace (5.8). In another passage Mechthild is quick to criticize beguines who exhibit this false holiness because they no longer tremble before God. Instead they enter worship out of blind habit. Mechthild accuses them of the worst in self-conceit. She admonishes them with a story of souls in hell who are asked why the reconciliation of God in Christ is not enough to satisfy them. "Is it not of such value that you will be satisfied with it? Shocked at such presumption the souls return to the way of truth but remain in torment" (3.15). Jesus died, she suggests, because of the treachery of the world (4.28).

Only the second child, who sees its faults with open eyes, bears the potential to return to God's love (5.8). The point is not to exhibit false humility, but to admit that there is an honesty demanded of true love that calls for self-examination. The sublimeness of love must meet God in the "mirror of true knowledge" of one's worthlessness, of the suffering, and of the secret sins committed against one's lover. To appear sinless, Mechthild suggests, is to be robbed by vain honor and struck down by pride. When one goes to God with desire, shame of sin, flowing love, and humble fear, then God casts "radiance toward the soul," which "dissolves out of deeply felt love" (6.1). Such humility does not deny or sacrifice self. Here Mechthild defines pride not as love of self, but as will of self over another. It is sin because it denies the nature of free will of the other that is a necessary ingredient of any love. The dance of love is a constant struggle to overcome pride and will one's self for another. It is this understanding of love that waits for God, with a heavy heart.

THE SUFFERING OF LOVE

With the understanding of the true nature of love comes the experience of suffering, and the desolation of love. It is both a suffering for God caused by the persecution of love and a suffering by God due to the absence of love (5.25). Mechthild describes it as estrangement:

> Ah, blessed Estrangement from God, how bound I am to you in love! You strengthen my will in pain and make pleasant for me the difficult long wait in this miserable body. By whatever means I make myself more your companion, the more intensely and wondrously God falls over me. O Lord, in the depths of pure humility I cannot sink away from you; alas, in pride I easily stray away from you!
>
> But the deeper I sink,
> The sweeter I drink (4.12)

Suffering is a very real experience for Mechthild. Sprinkled through her writing there are remarks about persistent persecution and harassment by others. Mechthild notes that spiritual people hold her in persistent and vicious contempt (3.16) and tarnish her honor with gossip (4.2; 6.38). The church persecutes her, challenging the orthodoxy of her writing (6.36) and refusing to offer her communion (3.5). Near the end of her life Mechthild thanks God for not being conquered by her enemies. Yet she confesses that if she had lived much longer, she would lay herself "under their feet" (6.28). No wonder she refers to life on earth as living in exile (7.48).

Yet Mechthild is able to proclaim that God strengthens her will in suffering because she realizes that the price for the knowledge of God's love is rejection and persecution. As one who tries to live in the world, but not of it, Mechthild is familiar with the contrast between her spiritual life, with its freedom and mutual exchange, and the social reality of restriction and hierarchy. While it is beyond Mechthild's power to stop the persecution, it is in her power to overcome its control of her life. Ulrike Wiethaus argues that the struggle for Mechthild is to transform her suffering, so that she will not be vanquished by it and distracted from the freedom of love of God.[7]

In this task, Mechthild draws strength from Christ, who is one with us in our suffering. As she languishes over the problems in her community, Christ answers, "I fasted in the desert with them. I was tempted by the enemy with them. . . . I was nailed to the cross with them; for this reason they should suffer willingly and complain little about their troubles. . . . I arose from the dead; thus shall they always rise out of their failings. . . . I ascended into heaven by my divine power; there they shall follow me in all the power of these words" (7.53; also see 3.10; 1.29). Thus the story of the passion and resurrection becomes a way to describe the whole cycle of suffering that the soul endures. Through Christ, Mechthild can hope for victory over suffering because of his victory over crucifixion. The point is to turn suffering into affirmation of life, which she does by linking the suffering of the crucifixion with the victory of the resurrection. The power of the crucifixion allows Mechthild to integrate suffering into the experience of divine love and thus transform it. The nearer she comes to God, even through suffering, the greater and more wonderful God appears because suffering does not separate Jesus from the love of God.

But even Jesus suffers the agony of God's absence, crying, "My God, My God, why have you forsaken me?" (Matthew 27:46). And this leads to the other aspect of the suffering of love, the difficult experience of the absence of God. In longing, Mechthild begins to understand the freedom of love with its corresponding need to wait for her lover to appear. But as she grows older, this waiting becomes more than moments of temporary absence; it is the struggle to accept the true estrangement of God. "Lover, how can I do without you for so long?" Mechthild cries. "Lord, if you will not receive my complaint, I must again take up my sorrowing and wait and suffer both inwardly and outwardly" (7.31). Such refrains are common in the last chapters of Mechthild's writing, and they are always answered with the command to wait patiently. Fear and constancy become her friends (7.48) and Mechthild learns to accept even estrangement as part of the love of God. The more deeply she sinks, even into the realm of silence, the more sweetly she drinks of God.

With this reminder of sweetness, Mechthild has returned to her experience of God's love. It is an amazing depth of love that endures the presence and profound absence of God. To taste tenderness is not to have a relationship with God that is sweet and lovely, or even to long for such a love. The goal of the soul, Hollywood argues, is to be able to have a well-ordered will that can experience both the presence and absence of God with equal love. For Mechthild, suffering is a necessary consequence (what Hollywood calls a "marker") of love.[8] But it is never the means of love or of salvation. The constancy of love, with its mutuality and freedom, remains even in its absence. So even in the depths of unmixed humility, Mechthild can proclaim, "I cannot sink away from you" (4.12).

CONTEMPORARY REFLECTIONS

It is difficult to ponder what women like Mechthild can teach us about the process of being satisfied. In our longing for women who can serve as models of faith, it is tempting to romanticize Mechthild as a truly free woman who made her own way in the world, and to forget the persecution that she endured or the twenty years in which she tried to overcome her body in order to love God. While she is not one of the best known figures of Christian history, some have tried to make her a spokesperson for their own theories of faith. Carl Jung, for example, argued that Mechthild is one of the best examples of his theory of the integration of masculine and feminine in universal love.[9] Such attempts make Mechthild into an object of modern theory rather than a subject of Christian faith.

The truth of the matter is that her world is not our world. Mechthild would have a hard time understanding the kind of "have it all" mentality of modern-day Christians. I doubt that she would consider any of us spiritual people. Her Christian world with its tough choices of love of God or family is neither familiar nor appealing to us. If we try to identify Mechthild-like devotion in our midst we might liken her to someone like Mother Teresa, but that would be giving Mechthild the kind of saintly status that she did not possess in her own day. Instead, it would further remove Mechthild from our own experience of faith.

Rather, the task, as Nadia Lahutsky has pointed out, is to look for the touch points between Mechthild's world and our own.[10] Given that she was writing for the spiritual person of her day, the true seeker of God's love rather than the exceptional saint, does her experience have any insight as we try to build a theology that saves lives? The newfound interest in Mechthild's writing among Christian scholars suggests that there is something here worth pondering. One of the common claims is an appreciation for the "freshness" of her writing.[11] I too am struck by the originality with which she uses the language of her day to speak of the complexity of God's love. The more I read her work, the more I am impressed with a genuineness that comes through in her writing. She tells us of her joys and of her struggles, of her devotion and her desire to control, of her spiritual ecstasy and the struggles of her soul. Anyone who has been in love can see in Mechthild an authentic quest to love God.

An important aspect of atonement theology is thinking through the role of Christ in establishing this relation of love. Traditionally, the crucifixion has been seen as the paradigm of self-sacrifice that not only mediates but models the way to salvation. Mechthild has some interesting ideas about the role of suffering in the relation of love. First, she suggests that Christ suffers with us because of his human experience of pain and suffering. As our true love, he is present with us in the pain and suffering of our lives. Secondly, Christ transforms our suffering by showing us how his own suffering is transformed through the resurrection. Suffering does not effect salvation, but neither does it thwart salvation. Suffering is a consequence of sin in the world. It is the sin of the world that persecutes those who love God and the sin of inadequate trust that doubts the constancy of God's love. Atonement is not about modeling Christ's act of sacrificial love, but overcoming it as he overcame the crucifixion.

An interesting addition to the concept of atonement is Mechthild's idea of the role of Mary in salvation. Since love is of the essence of God, Mechthild rationalizes that God cannot live without one to love. While motherly love is unconditional, the relationship of lovers requires reciprocity. When humanity falls, this relationship is lost and Mary takes on the role of God's lover. Therefore, Mary becomes the model of faith as the true lover of God. It is difficult to consider what modern implications we can gain from this. In Mechthild's day devotion to Mary was a common aspect of Christian faith. In our day Mary takes on a much smaller role, especially in Protestant theology. Feminist theology is torn over the issue of reclaiming a role for Mary, either as the feminine dimension of the divine or as the epitome of Christian womanhood. But we can see how Mechthild's ideas about the longing of love fit with the experience of Mary more than the experience of Christ. In Mary, Mechthild finds the inherent will for the other that is the basic nature of humanity. That she builds on a woman as the model of faith helps her to believe in her own ability as a woman of faith to love God. At the very least, her theology should make us contemplate the role that Mary might play in a feminist theology of atonement that moves beyond the double standard of virgin/mother. Mary may be seen as less maiden or mother and more properly understood as wife and lover of God.

However, the key concept in Mechthild's theology is not suffering or Mariology, but the mutual longing of love. Emilie Zum Brunn argues that Mechthild prepares the way for modern spirituality with her themes of freedom and self-will.[12] Indeed there is something to be said for reclaiming the characterization of the divine-human relationship as a relation of lovers. A modern attempt at this very kind of theology is Sallie McFague's suggestion that we need to combine descriptions of God as our mother with ideas of God as our lover and friend.[13] Unlike Julian's discussion of God as our mother, Mechthild's ideas about relation with God suggest a grown-up kind of love. It is a symbiotic love, which recognizes the freedom of humanity as well as the mutual need for love. If God is love, which is a central claim of Christian faith, then it is appropriate to think of this love in terms of the most intense and important of human loves. It fits well with feminist theology's claim that to be is to be in relation. To be God is to be in a full and mutual relation with what God loves.

Such an understanding of God will challenge the characterization of God or of ourselves as having power over the other. Here Mechthild provides a fresh approach for thinking through the problem of atonement. Feminist theology has questioned the traditional understanding that we are saved from self-centered love by sacrificial love or from pride by self-sacrifice. Rather, many feminist theologians argue, women need to be saved from selflessness by a love of self. The way that Roberta Bondi phrases this is that she needed to get over the harmful idea of self-sacrifice and reclaim her identity as being created in the image of God.[14]

Mechthild shifts the discussion away from a definition of pride or sacrifice to a discussion of what interrupts the flow of love. If love is characterized by mutuality, freedom, and vulnerability, sin is the refusal to accept the freedom of the other and thus an attempt to control love. She calls it self-will, false holiness, or pride, but in doing so she redefines pride as control over the other rather than disregard of the other. Thus we can begin to articulate a theology of atonement that incorporates the feminist critique of sin as selfishness and salvation as self-sacrifice and yet realizes the human experience of both participating in and interrupting the flow of God's love.

As one student said to me after a presentation of Julian's theology, "What about the problem of human will? I don't know about you, but I don't always think about, let alone love, God." Nor do I. And Mechthild gives us language to talk about self-will as the freedom for or against the other. It is a freedom to love and to ignore God. It is not a question of love of self or love of God; it is a question of loving self in relation to or apart from relation to God. Here Mechthild provides a needed correction to the ideas of atonement based on the writing of Julian of Norwich. Julian provides the foundation for a feminist theology of atonement by questioning the traditional definition of atonement as satisfying God's justice and redefining atonement as being satisfied that God loves us. We are saved from thinking we are unlovable. In order to do this, she suggests that humanity is not only good but possesses a childlike devotion to God that is like a child's devotion to its mother. God loves us unconditionally, and we unconditionally seek God's love.

Mechthild shares this confidence in the natural goodness of humanity and the will of God for love, but adds a depth of understanding of love by incorporating a definition of free will that helps us understand not only the experience of the absence of God's love, but also the absence of our desire for love. Mechthild helps us clarify the truth about the complexity of human longing and love for God.

With this emphasis on freedom, Mechthild has a more modern ring than Julian, which is curious because Julian lived two hundred years after Mechthild. Bynum suggests that this may be due to the different life experiences of Julian and Mechthild.[15] While Julian lived a life of seclusion as a recluse, Mechthild's relative freedom as a beguine gave her more opportunity to be aware of freedom of will as well as its inherent dangers. Likewise,

Mechthild is aware of suffering in a different way than Julian. While Julian lived during the time of the plague and struggled with the traditional idea that suffering is a divine punishment, Mechthild experienced persecution and struggled to understand the role of suffering in the relation of love. Julian is more focused on how Christ effects our salvation, while Mechthild is more concerned with how Christ helps us understand the experience of our own salvation. Ulrike Wiethaus has shown that the religious imagery of women mystics moved away from the lover imagery of the early Middle Ages to mother and child imagery in the fourteenth century.[16] Mechthild and Julian, then, are typical of the mystical motifs of their day.

As we begin to look at women as sources for theology, we must redefine our notion of progress in history. The women of the early Middle Ages had more freedom and opportunity than women who lived in the later medieval period. Therefore, a theology that is based on medieval women's writing may well need to move backwards in history to find ideas of progress. Unlike male theologians, who built upon the work of their predecessors, women built upon their mystical experiences, which were shaped by the major spiritual motifs and historical circumstances of their day. Mechthild lived during a time of new opportunities and freedom for women and the flowering of love mysticism, while Julian lived during a time of increasing restriction and maternal imagery for God. Given these circumstances, it is not surprising that discussions of free will are found in Mechthild but are absent in Julian, or that the former seems more modern to us than the latter. Our task is not to show how they build upon each other, but how we can build upon them. Together their writing offers insights for a contemporary theology that we must piece together out of the fragments of their thoughts.

A feminist theology of atonement is based on the premise that the human need for salvation is being satisfied that God loves us. Mechthild helps us to understand that to accept and participate in the flowing love of God is a complex and ongoing struggle. Sin plus love plus sacrifice does not lead to salvation. Rather, freedom plus love plus will for the other equals satisfaction, and that is salvation.

But what does it mean to participate in the flowing love of God? While the focus in the first two chapters has been on understanding atonement in terms of the love of God, our study would not be complete without a redefinition of the role of love of others, the place of work in the Christian life. While a recluse, Julian prayed for the concerns of her community and counseled Christians. As a beguine, Mechthild likely was engaged in works of Christian service in Magdeburg. From these two examples it is evident that the satisfied life is a life in which the love of God flows through oneself to the world. We now turn to the question of the role of work in a feminist theology of atonement. Here the amazingly prolific writer, composer, artist, and abbess Hildegard of Bingen will be our guide.

✕ ✕ ✕

chapter four

HILDEGARD OF BINGEN ON
SATISFYING WORK

Our study began with a look at the writing of Julian of Norwich to reflect on how God in Christ accomplishes our salvation. Then we considered Mechthild of Magdeburg in order to discuss the experience of that salvation. Now we turn to the writings of Hildegard of Bingen to think through our response to salvation. As discussed thus far, my hypothesis is that the doctrine of atonement provides a basic principle of the gospel that feminist theology needs to ponder anew: that we do not save ourselves. Atonement addresses the human need to be satisfied that God loves us and that this satisfaction is a divine action of saving love. It is experienced as a human longing that has to confront the freedom of love and the corresponding struggle to overcome self-will and desire for control. Freedom plus love plus the will for the other equals satisfaction.

But does this sound too individualistic? Is salvation just a "me and my God" relationship? Should not a doctrine of atonement talk about what we are saved for in addition to what we are saved from and whom we are saved by? A theology of atonement needs to clarify that we are not saved by our work, but that because of our salvation we are saved for the satisfying work of loving our neighbor and the world. The doctrine of atonement provides the foundation for a theology of satisfying work.

To think through these ideas, we turn to one of the hardest-working Christians of all time, Hildegard of Bingen. Born in 1098, she was put into a Benedictine community at the age of eight and spent her life as a nun, rising to the role of abbess and founding two new Benedictine communities. In addition to overseeing the construction and maintenance of these convents, she was an active leader of the Gregorian reform and embarked on four preaching tours in her sixties. During her eighty-one years she saw the investiture controversy, the first and second crusades, the rise of scholasticism, and the rise of heretical groups such as the Cathars. Hildegard read these factors as signs of spiritual decline and dedicated her life to calling people back to the ways of God. She was known in her own day as a prophet, and wrote letters to secular and religious leaders advising them on spiritual matters. Pope Eugene III wrote to Hildegard, "We are of the conviction that your soul glows so much with the fire of divine love that you lack no incentive for good action."[1]

For us the most important part of this good action is her written work. In addition to volumes of music, she wrote a morality play, books on medicine, books on saints' lives, and three volumes of theology entitled *Scivias* (*Know the Ways of God*), *The Book of the Rewards of Life*, and *Book of Divine Works*.[2] The first is the most traditionally theological, outlining the history of salvation. The second is more practical and personal, describing the virtues and vices of the Christian life. The third is a natural theology, discussing the human and natural order of the cosmos. Together these three works are a comprehensive theological summa. To know the ways of God is to know of the interdependence of all things as the work of God. As Caroline Bynum notes, Hildegard's focus is on the "place of the human person in a divine plan that marches from creation through Christ's incarnation to last judgment and final redemption."[3] She therefore outlines the cosmic structure of salvation with an eye toward teaching her readers how to live within the grand work of God.

The way that she outlines this structure is neither logical nor systematic. Influenced by her monastic setting, her work is symbolic, steeped in the images of Scripture, but not the formal logic of theologians. In a letter to Guibert of Gembloux she confesses, "I am not taught to write as philosophers do."[4] Instead, Hildegard is taught to write through visions. "Like a burning flame," she writes in a letter to Bernard of Clairvaux, "the vision moves my heart and soul and teaches me the depths of the interpretation."[5] She literally sees pictures that give her insight into the nature of Christian doctrine. Her writing describes these visions and the many layers of theological meaning that they represent.

In her time, it was crucial to claim visions as the source of her authority. Hildegard lived in a day when it was not accepted for women to teach, let alone write theology. By claiming visionary authority, Hildegard, like many other women mystics, was able to claim that her ideas were not her work, but came from God. At the age of forty-two, Hildegard experienced a vision in which God called her to write. She responded by writing *Scivias*. Her letter to Bernard was a plea for his support of her calling. He in turn sent some of her work to Pope Eugene, who read it aloud at the Council of Trier in 1147–1148. The council approved of her writing because of the soundness of her doctrine and because she did not claim to be writing in her own voice. Therefore, the church could hold to the rule that women had no authority to write or teach and still affirm the authority of Hildegard's theology.

The irony is that Hildegard was able to be accepted because she did not base her ideas on Scripture or tradition, but on her visions and their interpretations. While her work is filled with scriptural references, they are clearly used to correspond with the claims made in her visions. The result is a construction of theology that is not centered in past theological tradition. Written outside the mainstream theological context, her work is original in both form and content. It is this originality that has led to her current popularity. As Sabina Flanagan notes, while the "wave of scholasticism has long since peaked," aspects of Hildegard's thought have enduring value.[6] Now her work is part of our tradition and becomes a rich resource for our theological thinking.

THE STRUCTURE OF SALVATION

To gain wisdom from Hildegard's theology is no easy task. In addition to the usual problems of translating the mystical world of the Middle Ages to the postmodern world of today, Hildegard is the epitome of the nonsystematic thinker. It is not just that she has no order to her vast amount of writing, but also that the idea of deductive logic is contrary to the purpose of her work. Salvation for Hildegard is not to be conceptualized as a linear progression of history but as a cyclical or spiral movement of creation.[7]

Part 3 of the *Scivias*, entitled "The Edifice of Salvation," opens with an image of God sitting on a throne above a circle (SC, 3.1.1; see illustration 1). Here Hildegard envisions salvation as a circle of creation that begins and ends in the justice of God. God's power and work encircle the cosmos and

ILLUSTRATION 1

The One Sitting Upon the Throne. Reprinted by permission from
Hildegard of Bingen: Scivias, translated by Mother Columba Hart and Jane Bishop
(New York: Paulist Press, 1990), 307.

include every creature. In describing this vision Hildegard writes that God "wheels" around from the East, where justice originates, to the North, where the devil is conquered, to the West, where death is overcome, and to the South, where God's justice burns in the hearts of the faithful, finally returning again to the East. God completes the circuit of the world, thus perfecting the work of salvation (*SC*, 3.1.10).

Yet God sits on a throne, symbolizing God's immutable presence. In another passage Hildegard describes this presence as encircling love. "For the shape of the world exists everlasting in the knowledge of the true Love which is God. . . . The Godhead is like a wheel, a whole" (*D*, 2.2). To think of salvation in this way breaks open our usual approach of deciding which comes first, God's saving work or our response. Here the whole process is the circle of God at work in the world and the task is not to figure out cause and effect, but to see the pieces of salvation as creating a whole. It is to find our center in the work of God.

In this picture justice plays a crucial role as the endpoints of creation. God wheels from the East, where justice originates, and returns to the rising of justice in the East. Heinrich Schipperges suggests that Hildegard understands justice as the creating of social order. In the human realm it means "leaving each person his or her own space and respecting the other person."[8] As the work of God it is described as the scales that equitably weigh good and bad (*SC*, 3.4.21). Hildegard repeatedly talks about this scale in relation to the end of history, the point being that the vision of future justice serves as a guide for present moral action (*SC*, 3.12.10). She even compares justice to the liver because it serves as a filter that helps us to absorb good and purge evil from our souls (*D*, 3.10). In both human action and divine work, justice serves to help us order ourselves in relation to the whole of creation.

Hildegard uses the biblical image of the lost coin (Luke 15: 8–10) to give an example of God's justice at work. Humanity is the lost coin and Christ is the burning lamp, the Sun of Justice. God uses this lamp to sweep the house of history and find lost humanity. As in Jesus' parable, God calls together friends and neighbors, which Hildegard names as earthly deeds of justice and spiritual virtues. "Rejoice with Me in praise and joy," God proclaims, "for I have found [humanity], who had perished by the deception of the Devil" (*SC*, 3.3.20; also see *SC*, 3.13.9). Again the focus is on the saving work of God celebrated by justice and virtue, and illumined by Christ. Together this work serves to save lost humanity and restore wholeness to creation.

THE FALL AS LACK OF VIRTUE

The uniqueness of Hildegard's vision of salvation becomes even more pronounced when she describes how humanity became lost in the first place. While Hildegard discusses the Fall in the traditional form of Adam eating the apple of creation (*D*, 1.14; *R*, 2.46), an original description is found in *Scivias* (Book 2, Vision 1, entitled "the Redeemer"), in which she recasts sin as not plucking the flower of obedience (see illustration 2).

The predominant image in this vision is the same circle of God's creative justice hovering over the world and extending down into creation. Six circles represent the six days of creation. At the endpoint of God's creative power is the head of a human being rising from the clay of the earth. But then, Hildegard tells us, she sees this same flaming power offer the human a white flower. Up in the right-hand corner is this human, who smells the flower, turns away, and falls into a thick darkness (*SC*, 2.1.intro).

In describing the importance of this vision, Hildegard identifies the flower as the "sweet precept of obedience," which the human being failed to touch or eat. "For he tried to know the wisdom of the Law with his intelligence, as if with his nose," she writes, "but did not perfectly digest it by putting it in his mouth, or fulfill it in full blessedness by the work of his hands" (*SC*, 2.1.8). By turning away from the divine command, the human sinks into the gaping mouth of death, becoming entangled in many vices and failing to seek God by faith or by works.

This surprising imagery recasts the Fall as a sin of omission, a failure to act, rather than a rebellious action. Sin is not participating in the fullness of God's good creation by refusing the gifts offered by God. The point is that we are not created to merely admire the work and wisdom of God. We are called to eat of it. Thus nourished, we can engage in the work of God in the world. But failing in this action, the human starts a chain reaction of death and darkness that spreads throughout the world.

In another passage the image of the flower as the goodness of creation returns to clarify the nature of sin as not only inaction but as any action done without regard for our place in creation. Hildegard now sees a man picking the flowers off a huge tree and proclaiming that he possesses all the greenness of the world. He says, "I will hang onto the beauty of this world as long as I can. I do not understand words spoken about another life when I have never seen it." Immediately the tree dries up and the figure falls into darkness. The pillar of heavenly harmony proclaims, "I do not reject life, but I do trample

ILLUSTRATION 2

The Redeemer. Reprinted by permission from *Hildegard of Bingen:
Scivias*, translated by Mother Columba Hart and Jane Bishop
(New York: Paulist Press, 1990), 147.

all the sins underfoot. . . . You however, run around in the dark and work fee-bly with your hands" (*R*, 1.2). Clearly sin is not just the absence of work, but any failure to connect our work to the harmony and balance of God. Whether it is flowers we fail to eat or flowers we try to possess, it is the fail-ure to see our work as part of God's creation.

Therefore, sin not only affects us; it disrupts the order of creation. Hildegard writes that when Abel was murdered "the entire Earth sighed and at that moment was declared a widow: Just as a woman without the comfort of her husband remains fixed in her widowhood, the Earth was also robbed of its holy totality by the murder committed by Cain" (*D*, 2.47). To think of sin as robbing the earth of its wholeness underscores the social nature of sin in its cosmic dimensions. Sin destroys the fabric of God's creation.

Hildegard sees the darkness of death expanding to fill the whole of cre-ation. And so the whole of creation is called to respond to the darkness created by sin. Stars begin to appear in the darkness, growing in number and intensity. Then a great star shoots a ray toward the creative flame of God, which ignites a radiance in the earth. At the same time there appears from the earth a radi-ant man who absorbs the darkness of death in his body. Thus he "strikes the darkness such a strong blow that the person who is lying in it is touched by Him, takes on a shining appearance and walks out of it upright" (*SC*, 2.1.13).

The chain reaction of death and darkness that affects the whole of cre-ation now calls forth a chain reaction of light and salvation. The stars repre-sent Abraham, Isaac, Jacob, and the prophets, culminating in John the Baptist, who through their works of faith drive back the darkness in the world. The incarnation completes this chain as the flaming power of God rises from the womb of Mary. Christ, shown as a figure of gold, enlightens the world with his radiance. His figure fills Hildegard's vision and from his head shoot flames of light up into the darkness. Our eyes focus on his outstretched hand and the corresponding hand of the fallen human reaching out for his touch.

The overall impression is of the incarnation encompassing the earth and breaking into the darkness with the moment of salvation close at hand. Creation and redemption become one in the creative work of God. The interdependence of the entire cosmos is damaged by the fallenness of human-ity, and the world groans in travail for the work of Christ. It suggests a "keen sense of our sinfulness and our need for redemption through the saving action of Christ," while at the same time highlighting the crucial role of human work for the well-being of the whole of creation.[9] In it all the pieces of creation and salvation, the stars, the earth, the human, the savior, the Creator, the flowers, work together to form a whole.

THE SACRAMENTAL NATURE OF ATONEMENT

But this vision of atonement leaves us wondering how the saving touch of Jesus illumines our lives. The answer can be found in another vision, which picks up the drama of salvation at the moment when Christ absorbs death into his body. It is the sixth vision of Book 2, entitled "Christ's Sacrifice and the Church" (see illustration 3). The vision is divided into two parts. In the top portion we see a hand pointing to Christ on the cross. Standing beside him is a woman holding a chalice filled with the blood from Christ's wound. In the lower frame this same woman kneels beside the altar upon which the cross rests and looks up to see scenes from Christ's life reflected in mirrors around the table.

The woman represents the church. She is clothed in wedding garments depicting her role as the bride of Christ joined to him at the cross. The blood that flows from his wound is the dowry of her wedding. A voice from heaven declares, "May she, O Son, be your Bride for the restoration of My people; may she be a mother to them, regenerating souls through the salvation of the Spirit and water" (SC, 6.1.intro). Again Hildegard reminds us that salvation is a social reality. The bride of Christ is not an individual soul but the community of the church, born at the moment of his passion. Through this community we enter into the relationship of salvation.

We receive this saving relationship through the sacrament of communion. As Barbara Newman notes, Hildegard sees atonement from a sacramental rather than a sacrificial point of view.[10] The hand in the upper corner holds a scroll with the words of the mass that bring the mystery of the salvation of spirit and water down to the altar of the church. A voice from heaven declares, "Eat and drink the body and blood of My Son to wipe out Eve's transgression, so that you may be restored to the noble inheritance" (SC, 2.6.intro). The bread of communion is likened to true medicine that heals our injustice and gives us "supernal strength" (SC, 2.6.21; SC, 2.6.22). "Now we are satisfied," Hildegard writes, "for we drink in Him the saving cup, tasting Who God is in true faith" (SC, 2.6.29).

The nature of this God becomes clear as we look at the scenes of Christ's life portrayed in the mirrors above the table. Here we see the birth, death, resurrection, and ascension of Christ. The crucifixion is framed within the con-

ILLUSTRATION 3

Christ's Sacrifice and the Church. Reprinted by permission from
Hildegard of Bingen: Scivias, translated by Mother Columba Hart and Jane Bishop
(New York: Paulist Press, 1990), 235.

text of Christ's entire life. Newman notes that throughout her work Hildegard makes the virgin birth at least as important as the cross.[11] In fact, Hildegard always depicts the crucifixion in the midst of the total life of the incarnation and the community of faith. Hildegard writes that the passion of Christ is analogous to his birth as confirmation is to our baptism (SC, 2.4.8). For both the Christian and Christ it is not an event but the whole life of faithful response to God that is the point. When we look at Christ's life in its entirety, Hildegard suggests, we see that he saves by humility and justice, not power and strength. It is not a picture of a fighter who conquers in a moment of power, but of great goodness and humility that shines throughout a whole life (SC, 2.6.3).

By envisioning the life of Christ in its entirety, the sacrament of communion strengthens us for works of justice in the life of faith. He awakens in us "splendid virtues" pleasing to God (SC, 2.6.21). Those who "faithfully cleave to Him," Hildegard writes, "are made by Him green and fruitful, so that they bring forth noble fruits of virtue; as He too, being sweet and mild, brought forth precious offshoots in holiness and justice" (SC, 2.6.28). The purpose of communion is to remember this saving work and to be restored to our own place in it. As Rosemary Radford Ruether notes, for Hildegard the act of restoration culminates in Christ, who takes on human flesh and restores the original form of humanity as the perfect receptive instrument of the divine spirit. Christians share this restored human nature through rebirth into the womb of mother church and through feeding on the sacrament of Christ's body in communion.[12]

By viewing atonement as a sacramental act, Hildegard links the divine action of atonement to the human response of faith. She sees people coming to the altar to receive the sacrament in different modes of faith. Some are bathed in brilliance, seeing in the mirror of Christ's life the restoration of their own humanity; others come in a cloud darkened by their own deeds of injustice and their lack of faith in the saving work of Christ (SC, 2.6.57). Clearly, the message is that our ability to be saved by the work of Christ is linked to how we are saved for the work of God in the world. Touched by the brilliance of salvation, we are left to enlighten the world through our lives of virtue.

SATISFYING WORK

Now it becomes clear that the purpose of salvation is to plant virtues in the soul. In the tenth vision of the third part of *Scivias*, Hildegard sees Christ sitting on the throne of justice surrounded by five virtues (see illustration 4). Behind the throne we see the circle of God's creative spirit of justice grasped by the right hand of Christ. Before him are five women who stand at his command. These are the virtues who symbolize "potent divine energies working for good in the cosmos and in human souls."[13] In the middle stands Constancy with a deer on her chest. To her right is Desire, who focuses her gaze on the deer. The deer is another symbol for the Son of God, and Hildegard quotes Psalm 41:2. "As a hart pants after the water-brook, so my soul pants after you, O God" (SC, 3.10.11). To the left is Compunction (better translated as Longing), who looks through the windows in Constancy's chest for the presence of God. Together, Constancy, Desire, and Compunction show the love of God, which is the focus of all work done to build up the city of justice.

Below is Contempt of the world set within the circle of divine compassion and to the right is Harmony, shining so brightly in the vision of God's peace that her face is obscured by illumination. Contempt proclaims, "for the fountain of salvation has drowned Death, and poured its stream into me to make me blossom in redemption" (SC, 4.10.13). One such blossom is held in her hand. The effect of partnering Contempt with Harmony is to show Contempt as the power of discernment, striving for the balance of work, prayer, and study that are the hallmarks of the Benedictine life. Works of justice blossom in the discerning Christian life.

Looking back to Christ, we see that he sits on top of a stairway of seven steps. Along with the seven days of creation, these steps show a stairway between God and human action. Good works descend upon people from God, Hildegard writes, and the glory of God shines in the good works. Thus works of justice serve as ornaments of the holy city of justice (SC, 4.10.31). In addition, these works link us to God. "When people begin to do good works with a calm and bright intention, they touch God" (SC, 3.10.28). The touch of God that was symbolized in the illumination of the incarnation and the birth of the church in the crucifixion is now completed through the work of human hands.

In another passage Hildegard sees a ladder of virtues that descend in Christ's humanity and ascend in his divinity, then flow down again to the hearts of the faithful and through him to works in the world (SC, 3.8.13). The fluidity of the work of God in and through human hands shows both divine grace and human cooperation in the work of salvation. Newman calls this the synergy of atonement.[14] Since we view such ideas through the eyes of

ILLUSTRATION 4

The Son of Man and the Five Virtues. Reprinted by permission from
Hildegard of Bingen: Scivias, translated by Mother Columba Hart and Jane Bishop
(New York: Paulist Press, 1990), 471.

the Reformation, it is important to note that this is not a salvation by works. Hildegard explicitly states that this is not a justification by works of law grounded in the old way of sacrifice but is a life of works of love planted in faith in Christ (R, 2.25). Therefore she can proclaim, "I find all satisfaction in virtues and faithfully climb from virtue to virtue" (D, 2.19). This is not a scrambling search for salvation that we associate with works righteousness, but a confidence and joy in the ability to touch God because the glory of God shines in good works.

Returning to the image of the flower, Hildegard now talks about our lives as blooming in salvation. She likens the soul to a good field carefully prepared by grace to bloom in greenness. "To a person who willingly and with good heart receives the seed of My word, I grant the gifts of the Holy Spirit in superabundance, as to a good field" (SC, 3.10.4). While salvation rains upon us from above and Christ awakens holiness in a person and sets it growing, it is up to us to "labor in the field of our heart" to cultivate salvation (SC, 3.10.5; SC, 3.1.intro). In her *Book of Divine Works* Hildegard picks up this theme, describing the goal of the Christian life as becoming "gardens in bloom," like an "orchard full of the fruits of good works" (D, 4.82). Robert Olson notes that "in the *Scivias* she tells us that if humans fulfill their responsibility and cultivate the fields, they will produce crops; no more is necessary because God has infused the seeds with *viriditas* [greenness]. Similarly, if humans, for whom God is responsible, act virtuously, keeping the Word of God and observing the sacraments of the Church, they will find salvation."[15]

It is this theme of *viriditas*, or greenness, that unites Hildegard's understanding of salvation. While we saw that sin is abusing or ignoring greenness, the sacrament of communion makes us green, and in good works our souls bloom green. Greenness is symbolized by the flower, which is offered in creation by God and rejected by fallen humanity, yet held in the hand of virtue redeemed by Christ. In other texts Hildegard describes mercy and justice as green (R, 1.8; 2.27), the soul as the green life-force of the flesh (D, 4.21), the Holy Spirit as the moisture of greenness (R, 5.76), the virgin Mary as providing the flesh of greenness to the Son of God (R, 6.45), and Jesus as the green wood that causes the greening power of the virtues (D, 10.19).

Many scholars have commented on the importance of the image of greenness in the work of Hildegard. Peter Dronke notes that greenness is an important symbol for overcoming the dualism between earthly and heavenly existence. Whereas the Cathars denied earthly life, Hildegard's use of the symbol of greenness confirms everyday life as good and of God. Furthermore, Gregory the Great, one of the few Christian writers who mentions greenness, used the idea as an image of spiritual health.[16] Thus Hildegard was able to identify her thought with that of Gregory and counter the heresy of the Cathars.

In any event, the effect is to highlight our place in the chain of being as creatures who receive greenness from creation and from the saving work of God and give it back to creation through works of virtue. I agree with Rita Brock that the vision of salvation that Hildegard gives us is one of the "greening of the soul."[17] We are saved in order to grow in the fullness of life and goodness and take our rightful place in the grand scheme of God.

CONTEMPORARY REFLECTIONS

How can Hildegard provide insight for our earlier questions about atonement? How can she help to deepen the conviction that we do not save ourselves and at the same time give insight into thinking through the social reality of salvation? Is it possible to talk about the satisfying work of atonement without returning to the idea that we are satisfying God?

The first idea worth exploring is the way in which Hildegard connects the doctrine of atonement to the sacrament of communion. To refocus atonement as a sacramental rather than sacrificial act stresses the practical aspect of atonement within the context of worship. It reminds us that atonement is the present work of God rather than the past event of crucifixion. As Julian noted, Christ nourishes us in communion and it is this nourishment and the fellowship of the church that perform the healing work of God. At communion, we see the birth, death, resurrection, and ascension of Christ as part of the saving work of God. We are called to the table to eat of the flower of God's wisdom, and digest it. Thus nourished, we can rise to the satisfying work of love.

This sacramental framework for atonement helps us to make sense of the passion without reinforcing the destructive notion that we save ourselves through modeling Christ's self-sacrifice. Julian reminds us that Christ satisfies us—not the other way around—and Mechthild suggests that Christ finds satisfaction in overcoming suffering rather than dwelling in it. In addition, Hildegard provides a vision of atonement that is centered on a holistic view of Christ. While much of feminist theology and contemporary theology in general has focused solely on the incarnation, whereas most of the classical tradition focused solely on the crucifixion, Hildegard focuses on the whole life of Christ from virgin birth to ascension.

The centrality of circles in Hildegard's visions reinforces a nonlinear conception of atonement. Julian's insight begins with the realization that the Fall and the incarnation are coterminous events. Such a view refocuses salvation as an existential state of being rather than as a historical event. Mechthild provides a deeper understanding of the existence of salvation. To be in relationship with God requires a centering of self that realizes the full depth of one's freedom and self-control. But it is Hildegard who enlarges our vision to see how the relationship between oneself and God rests within the cosmic order of God's creation.

This focus helps us break the individualistic trend in atonement theology. A key idea in Hildegard's understanding of atonement is the interdependent nature of the cosmos. The chain reaction of sin and salvation helps us see our important role in the building of God's city of justice. The sin of humanity spreads darkness throughout the world. Individual acts of sin, such as the murder of Abel, wound the earth. Likewise, the touch of Christ heals fallen humanity by absorbing the power of darkness into his body and illuminating the world with light. The presence of the church passes that touch on to us, and as we respond in acts of virtue, we touch God. It is not self-sacrifice that is the point of Christ's life or ours; it is works of justice that complete the circle of creation.

This return to the idea of justice is necessary in order to address the way in which salvation not only heals us but reconciles the world to God. Anselm highlights justice and with it the importance of the social nature of the doctrine of atonement. His understanding of justice, however, is at the expense of an understanding of the satisfying love of God. Julian provides the paradigm shift to the relationship of love, but does so at the expense of a concern for justice. Mechthild clarifies that this relationship is an interrelationship between God and humanity, but does not see beyond that interpersonal experience. Given her role as abbess and church reformer, Hildegard does highlight the importance of justice and order (which is Anselm's real concern) as a necessary ingredient in a doctrine of atonement. The circle of creation begins and ends in the East, which is the seat of justice, because of the interdependence of life. Here Hildegard gives fresh insight to justice as bringing creation together in wholeness. The sin of not finding and living out one's place in the world begins a chain reaction of sin that darkens the cosmos.

Likewise, the light of Christ flows into the world, bringing it back to the fullness and greenness of life. With justice goes an appropriate role for judgment because our work has an effect on the whole of creation.

This brings us back to the main theme of satisfaction. My claim is that Anselm's idea of satisfaction implies that atonement is a divine need. Anselm argues that humans cannot offer satisfaction, but we ought to, seemingly because we need to restore the honor stolen from God. Hildegard's vision of the ladder of virtue shows the restoring of order as a two-way affair. This restoration travels from the humanity of Christ to his divinity, back down to our humanity, and up again to God. In the process, the order—and I might add the honor—of the cosmos is satisfied. Hildegard focuses on human action from the moment of the Fall, envisioned as a failure to act, yet it is clear that our good works are not the cause of our satisfaction. Rather, it is the presence of Christ in communion that satisfies us and the touch of God that we experience in our good works.

Thus, Hildegard builds on the understanding of power that has been implicit throughout this study. Julian questions the wrath of God as an example of divine power over creation. She suggests instead that the real power of God is the power of courtesy. The eternal and omnipresent vision of God can see beyond the limited vision of the servant and see creation in its created, fallen, and redeemed states. God's power works in creation through Christ to empower us with a glimpse of eternal love. She suggests that real power is the power of friendship and Mechthild picks up this theme in her poetry of longing and love. The vulnerability of power with its longing and freedom confronts us not only with a new vision of God, but a deepened vision of our power to be free from or free for that power in our lives. With Hildegard we see how the power of creation moves back and forth between God, Christ, and the work of virtue. Through such work we tap into the divine power and thus are satisfied. After all, we "touch God."

Self-sacrificial love does not overcome sin. Such acts are based in a lack of understanding of the nature of sin and the mistaken impression that sacrifice will bring us back into the circle of God's love. Rather, self-satisfying work is empowered by confidence in the love of God and points us forward to the completion of God's circle of creation. Atonement is the life of satisfaction.

✳ ✳ ✳

PART TWO

LIVING A SATISFIED LIFE

chapter five

MARGERY KEMPE ON SEARCHING
FOR THE SATISFIED LIFE

As a member of the admissions committee at my seminary, I have the pleasure of interviewing potential students. While the details of their lives differ, they all share a common search for more out of life. Some talk of realizing that their current career is unfulfilling and of hoping that service to the church will provide a more satisfying way of life. Others talk about experiences in local churches or summer camps that have given them a vision of a satisfying life. A few have had their lives touched by moments of amazing grace and are searching for a way to respond. All come to seminary not only to reflect on their faith but to begin to live satisfying lives.

How do you live a satisfied life? It is one thing to think through the meaning of atonement as the satisfying love of God; it is another to see it in action in the life of Christian faith. The goal is not just to be atoned, but to live an atoning life. The first part of this work suggests that atonement is the human need to be satisfied that God loves us. As we understand the nature of the satisfying love of God, we are drawn into the world to live in love. To enter this world, we need not only to understand the nature of atonement but also to see how atonement is experienced in models of faith. This section will focus not on the ontology of satisfaction but on living the satisfied life in the Middle Ages as well as today.

Julian might seem a likely model, since she is the one who understood best the nature of atonement as satisfying love. Unfortunately, we know little about the details of her life. The one thing that we do know is that she was an anchoress who lived a life of seclusion and reflection, a life that is far removed from our modern practice of faith. Yet Julian provided guidance to a medieval laywoman who wrote a detailed account of her own life of faith. This woman, Margery Kempe, sought counsel from Julian. Her search was the result of an amazing moment of grace. After the birth of her first child, Margery experienced a severe depression and was called back to sanity by a mystical experience of God's accepting love. Years later she received a call to a religious vocation but struggled with how to lead a religious life as a wife and mother. Margery needed confirmation that her desire for a more satisfying life, and the increasing fits of weeping that accompanied it, were not delusions. Julian assured her that her tears of contrition, devotion, and compassion came from God and were confirmations of the presence of the Holy Spirit in her soul. She urged Margery to be steadfast in right faith. "I pray God grant you perseverance. Set all your trust in God and do not fear the talk of the world, for the more contempt, shame, and reproof that you have in this world, the more is your merit in the sight of God. Patience is necessary for you, for in that shall you keep your soul" (1.18).[1]

Margery followed Julian's advice to persevere. Born in 1373 in the town of King's Lynn in Norfolk, England, she was the daughter of a prominent citizen, John Burnham. She married John Kempe at the age of twenty and settled into married life. After recovering from the trauma of her first child's birth, she had thirteen more children. The next twenty years were spent in the usual duties of caring for a family in the emerging town of Lynn. But she was not satisfied with her life and longed for a closer relationship to God. Later she had a vision of Christ calling her to a mystical marriage. In her day such a call was understood as a call from married life to celibate life in Christ. While celibate marriage was not unheard of in her day, it required the consent of her husband, which was not forthcoming. She turned to other practices of lay devotion such as weeping and fasting. In 1413 she negotiated a chastity agreement with her husband and began a life of pilgrimage to religious sites. She traveled to Rome, Jerusalem, and Spain to visit the sites of Christian leaders of faith. In her late fifties she returned to Lynn to care for her husband until his death, after which she embarked on one more pilgrimage to Europe. Through it all she searched for a way to respond to the satisfying love experienced in her moment of need.

The story of her life is recorded in her autobiography, *The Book of Margery Kempe*. Written in 1436–1438, it was rediscovered in 1940 as the first autobiography written in the English language. It has received a lot of scholarly attention for its historic nature but, as Julian feared, it has also endured "much talk." The book is not a chronology of Margery's life and is not really an autobiography by modern standards; it is the story of Margery's religious quest. Prone to bouts of weeping and confrontations with church leaders, Margery is portrayed as a controversial figure who annoyed and baffled her contemporaries. Her book is filled with visions of God that are incredible to modern readers. The content of these visions stretches the limit of acceptable religious experience. Scholars have had a hard time fitting her into any category of mysticism and have often dismissed her as a "minor mystic" or even worse, a religious fraud. She is seen as inferior to the saintly Julian who pursued her religious vocation in a quiet and acceptable manner.

Yet it is the unique nature of Margery's life that makes her an interesting study of the search for satisfaction. She attempted to live a religious vocation in the midst of ordinary life. While women in continental Europe had been experimenting with new forms of Christian practice for 200 years, in England religious women were required to live enclosed lives as nuns or anchoresses. By the fourteenth century, however, a new mode of lay devotion was emerging in England. It was based on the devotion of women such as the beguines, who saw piety and chastity as ways to love God with one's whole heart. It followed the practice of the Franciscans, who popularized the idea that tears were a sign of piety and a means to salvation. The focus in both these groups was on affecting or moving the heart of the believer by reliving the events of Jesus' life. Julian did this by imagining the crucifixion; Margery did this by visiting the site of the crucifixion. Tears, pilgrimage, and chastity were means to a deeper compassion and personal transformation.[2]

Margery also lived during a time of religious and political unrest in England. It was the beginning of the end of the medieval era. In Lynn the feudal system was transforming into a capitalist culture. Religious dissidents began challenging church authority. In 1378 the pope censured John Wyclif, but a group called the Lollards continued his critique. Lollards were considered a threat to social order because they advocated individual interpretation of the Scriptures and withholding of church tithes. In response Archbishop Arundel banned translation of the Bible into English, criticism of the sacraments, and possession of Wyclif's works. Lollards were burned at the stake. It was a climate in which the church feared heresy and yet allowed a wide range of religious individuality as long as one did not support Lollard practices. Not surprisingly, Margery was often accused of being a Lollard, but she managed to defend herself against the charges by walking a fine line between orthodox belief and heretical practice.

Given this context of lay piety and religious dissent, it is not surprising that Margery contemplated her own martyrdom. Fearing the worst from her critics, she imagined which kind of execution she could endure (her answer—beheading). In response, she heard the soothing voice of God calm her fears by promising to love her without end. She was told that God is as constant as the sun, sometimes bright and sometimes hidden by a cloud, but always near. Then Margery heard an affirmation of her gift of tears and a call to religious practice:

> When you strive to please me, then you are a true daughter; when you weep and mourn for my pain and my passion, then you are a true mother having compassion on her child; when you weep for other people's sins and adversities, then you are a true sister; and when you sorrow because you are kept so long from the bliss of heaven, then you are a true spouse and wife, for it is the wife's part to be with her husband and to have no true joy until she has his company. (1.14)

This text shows the search of Margery's life as a spiritual journey of growing awareness that sought to integrate her identities as a daughter, wife, and sister/mother through the practices of contrition, longing, and compassion. It was not a search for perfection or holiness, but for wholeness. It was a "holistic lifelong path on which a growing relationship with the Divine is coupled with a deepening love of self and neighbor."[3] It is as we further understand this path that we understand Margery's search for satisfaction.

THE SEARCH FOR SELF IN TEARS OF CONTRITION

Julian realized that being satisfied that God loves you is a difficult process. It involves wearing away feelings of unworthiness and replacing them with the realization of one's identity as a child of God. Julian named this process contrition (Margery used this word interchangeably with the word *compunction*). Julian wrote that this process begins when one is seized by the Holy Spirit, and it requires the healing of one's psychic wounds, reviving of the soul, and being restored to the life of the church (*SHL*, 39). The search for satisfaction is first and foremost a search for the acceptance of one's self as seen in the eyes of God.

Julian must have had Margery in mind when she wrote these words. Margery's greatest and constant fear was that she would be forsaken by God. Her fear was grounded in a profound sense of being forsaken in her moment of crisis by the church. Having endured a difficult first pregnancy, she lived to deliver her child, but "despaired of her life, believing she might not live." She called for a priest to confess a secret sin that she had never revealed, but before she could speak, the priest rebuked her. Fearing she would die in a state of damnation, Margery went mad. For six months she was so tormented that she had to be physically restrained. Then she received a vision of Christ, whom she heard say, "Daughter, why have you forsaken me, and I never forsook you?" (1.1). With this blessing, her fears subsided and Margery was restored to health.

The fear of being forsaken returned again and again in Margery's life. As she asked for penance, she received a vision of Christ, who promised never to forsake Margery in happiness or sorrow and granted her contrition until the end of her life (1.5). She experienced this contrition as a flame of the fire of love that burned away her sins (1.35). When she was deserted by friends, she heard God assure her that "although all your friends forsake you, I shall never forsake you" (1.63). Finally, even God became frustrated with her insecurity and proclaimed, "How often have I told you that your sins are forgiven you and that we are united together in love without end?" (1.22).

Margery had a hard time accepting forgiveness because she assumed that she had to please God. After all, she had been told that by pleasing God as a daughter she would be loved (1.14). As long as she carried the burden of her unworthiness this was an impossible task. Caught in the medieval world of penance and merit, Margery saw no satisfaction in trying to earn God's love. Realizing her dilemma, God answered her prayers with the insight that she could not please God better than by believing that she was loved. "The time shall come," God promised, "when you will consider yourself well pleased" (1.32).

Such a dramatic redefinition of the idea of pleasing God was hard for Margery to accept. Sometimes she was assured of God's love and acted as though no obstacle could overcome her. At other times she doubted God's love and was little pleased with herself. The most dramatic example of her struggle was a three-year period of temptation and despair. She came very close to adultery and was stopped only by the rejection of the man she desired. Ashamed and confused, her sense of unworthiness deepened and she mourned as though she had been forsaken by God (1.4). Another time when she was struggling with religious doubt about the justice of God, her imagination was captured by horrifying sexual fantasies. Angrily she cried, "Lord, you have said before you would never forsake me. Where is the truthfulness of your word?" (1.59). Once again doubt led to temptation and resulted in her feeling forsaken by God.

The sexual nature of her temptations suggests that at the core of Margery's struggle was the inability to accept herself as a wife and mother. She lived in an era that equated piety with chastity. While marriage was consecrated as an acceptable mode of Christian life, widowhood was understood as a more religious state, and maidenhood was the true mode of holiness. Thus it was logical for Margery to consider herself unworthy of God's love as long as she remained a wife and mother. Her despair was a result of the conflict of her identity as wife of John Kempe with her religious desire to be the daughter of God. To accept herself would require a reappraisal of her married state as a permanent state of unholiness.

Once again, she received a revelation that transformed her life. Fearing that she was pregnant, Margery was reassured that the birth of another child would not be a barrier to God. God took heed only of what she would become. While affirming the perfection of maidenhood, she was told that God loves wives, for no one can prevent God from loving whomever God desires. Love, God reminded Margery, quenches all sin. Being reminded of Mary Magdalene and Paul as sinners transformed by God's love, Margery realized the potential for her own life (1.21). Overcome by the sweetness of God's love, she wept tears of relief and joy.

Margery's transformation, like that of many seekers, took years and endured many setbacks. She began by realizing she could be a maiden in her soul (1.22) and worked to construct a new life as a pilgrim and a mystic. In Rome she completed the transformation of her identity from wife to maiden of God. In a confusing passage that names Margery as daughter, mother, and wife, God declared, "Daughter, there was never a child so kind to its mother as I shall be to you, both in joy and sorrow, to help you and comfort you. And that I pledge to you" (1.35). Back home in Lynn she received a vision of her name written in the Book of Life (1.85). With this confirmation, Margery was able to transcend the religious doubt that was typical of her day. Despair gave way to comfort; temptation was transformed into good faith.

An important aspect of this transformation was the support of advisors and friends. After being assured of God's faithfulness, Margery was commanded to seek out a Dominican anchorite for spiritual counsel, with the promise that God's spirit would speak through him (1.5). The anchorite's unwavering support of Margery was a crucial confirmation of her search for acceptance. He assured her that her feelings were "good and sure" (1.18) and refused to desert her even when his own reputation was threatened (1.19). Margery described him as "the most special and singular comfort" of her life because she knew he would never forsake her (1.69). Through his faithfulness Margery experienced the acceptance of God.

Unfortunately her confessor died before Margery's first pilgrimage, and she was left with the task of telling the story of her life over and over to potential advisors in the hope of seeking spiritual comfort. Without an advisor to support her, Margery had no one to help her interpret her unusual religious experiences or to defend her from criticism. This put her in the vulnerable position of having to defend herself. Typical of her encounters was her meeting with the vicar of Norwich, who initially insulted her but changed his mind when he heard her impressive story of faith. She left that conversation greatly strengthened and bolder in faith (1.17). Over and over she sought out kindred spirits, who comforted her, confirmed the validity of her actions, supported her against her critics, believed the sincerity of her devotion, and most importantly, listened to the story of her life (see 1.17; 1.27; 1.33; 1.69). Through this multitude of supporters she was able to gain the confidence to accept herself as loved by God.

Not surprisingly, her book ends with a return from Europe to seek her confessor's support. Having traveled against his advice, she was anxious to receive his forgiveness. After a few words of rebuke she received "as good love from him and other friends afterwards as she had before" (2.10). With this reconciliation, the damage done by her first confessor, who had rebuked and forsaken her, became a distant memory. Called out from despair by the comfort of God, affirmed through continued assurance, and supported by earthly advisors, Margery finally came home to her identity as the well-pleased daughter of God.

THE SEARCH FOR GOD IN TEARS OF DEVOTION

As Margery grew in her identity as the daughter of God, she desired to be closer to God. Though she began to accept her married status as a beginning point for her life, she longed for the kind of spiritual marriage described by beguines such as Mechthild. Like Mechthild, Margery was not satisfied with a dependency upon God, but sought an intimacy with God that transcended earthly limitations of tenderness and longing. Unfulfilled by the ordinary life of a laywoman, she admitted that "all the clerics that preach may not satisfy me, for I think that my soul is always just as hungry" (1.58). It was not enough to feel God's acceptance through the usual avenues of sacrament and the Word; she was hungry for the wholehearted devotion of God.

Her first glimpse of this deeper awareness of God came years after her near-death conversion. Having regained her health and resumed her duties as a housewife, she was living a normal—if unexceptional—life when she heard sweet music, which drew her from her bed to heaven. So profound was her experience of heavenly joy that afterwards she could talk of little else. Often described as her second conversion, this moment gave her a vision of a deeper devotion to God. She wrote that she was drawn toward God in an unforgettable manner. After this awakening, she annoyed her friends by her lack of concern for daily affairs and dismayed her husband by her confession that she had transferred all her love and affection from him to God alone (1.3).

The quest for celibacy was Margery's way of searching for more out of her relationship with God. Given the marital customs of the day, she could not divorce her husband. While she hoped and prayed for his consent to a chaste relationship, she increased her devotional practice in the form of fasting and confession and weeping. During this time she had momentary glimpses of God. On one such occasion, she reported that her spirit was "ravished" by Jesus (1.5), but in general her search for greater devotion was frustrated by the responsibilities of ordinary life. Finally, her relationship with her husband was strained to the breaking point. Together they negotiated a new relationship in which she promised to pay his financial debts and break her fast in exchange for a chaste marriage. Having consented to her desire to be wholly devoted to God, John affirmed her calling with the witty blessing, "May your body be as freely available to God as it has been to me" (1.11). While the arrangement is a bit bizarre by modern standards, Lynn Staley notes that Margery sought to conform all her relationships to her vision of heaven. The table fellowship of the reign of God was a natural successor to marital relations.[4]

Freed from her marital vows, Margery prayed for a mystical marriage to God. Her wish was fulfilled later that year as she worshiped in Rome. Having imagined a marriage to the youthful Christ, whom she caressed in the arms of her soul (1.36), she was at first reluctant to consider this proposal from the first person of the Trinity. In the end her desire for God overcame her romantic delusions. She imagined a wedding complete with the exchange of marriage vows in the presence of the Son, the Spirit, Mary, the apostles, and various saints. In a state of "high devotion" she records that she celebrated with heavenly company the joy of company with God (1.35).

In preparation for this new status, Margery changed her dress from the traditional robes of a medieval wife to the white clothes of virginity. The change of dress symbolized her willingness to profess her devotion to the world. (To declare her devotion to her husband was one thing, to expose her desire to the world, another.) She was commanded by God two different times over the course of a year to wear white. The first time she confessed that she feared the ridicule of people if she dressed differently (1.15). The second time she promised to change clothes once she arrived in Rome (1.30). After arriving safely, she honored her commitment (1.31). As expected, her clothes were a frequent source of controversy (see 1.34; 1.39; 1.48; 1.50; 1.52), but her willingness to make a public profession of her devotion was instrumental in transforming her from an ordinary wife to the wife of God.[5]

While white clothes were the outward sign of her devotion, pilgrimage was the means. It was in Rome that she made her devotion public and where she experienced her mystical marriage to God. Journeying away from her ordinary life provided Margery with the opportunity to leave her former responsibilities behind. While on the road she shed her identity as wife and mother and forged a new one as mystic and pilgrim. In order to feel closer to the presence of Christ, she traveled to Jerusalem, visiting the places where Christ walked. At Calvary the pain of the crucifixion was so real to her that people were amazed and astounded by her weeping (1.28). This experience of empathy marked a new level in her devotion that stayed with her for many years. Her purpose was not just to imitate Christ, but to actively devote herself to the love of God. "She traveled to extend her experience of the sacred."[6]

Her travels took her to all the well-known pilgrimage sites (Jerusalem, Rome, Compostela) and later to Norway. Along the way she searched for companions that could confirm and share her devotion. Like many pilgrims,

Margery included stops at the sites of Christian saints. While in Rome she visited the tomb of Jerome, who Julian had told her wrote in support of the piety of tears. Jerome appeared to Margery in a vision and blessed her crying as a special gift from God (1.41). Later she heard the apostle Paul apologize to her for the harm she had endured as a result of his writing about women (1.65).

While the confirmation of these important men increased her confidence, it was the example of women of faith that inspired her devotion. Key among them was Bridget of Sweden, whose life as a wife and mystic provided an important precedent for Margery's own quest. Margery was in Rome during the canonization hearings for Bridget. She visited the room where Bridget died and talked with her former maidservant in order to find out more about her life (1.39). While Bridget did not become a mystic until after her husband's death, she provided a model of an ordinary wife who had sought a life of greater devotion to God. In Assisi, Margery traveled the path where Angela of Foligno (another widow turned mystic) had begun her holy life of crying (1.31), and her last pilgrimage was to Danzig, where Dorothea of Montau had lived (2.4). Like Margery, Dorothea had married, had many children, experienced a spiritual calling, negotiated a chaste marriage, and become a pilgrim.

This spiritual cloud of witnesses became excellent travel companions for Margery. Unfortunately, her earthly companions were less inspiring. Her travels were filled with conflict, cruelty, and misunderstanding on the part of her companions. Refusing to join them in their feasting, Margery was ostracized from their company. In retaliation for her pious attitude, her companions tried to humiliate her by cutting her gown (1.26) and stealing her bedding (1.28). They threatened to leave her behind if she continued her fasting, weeping, and talk of holiness (1.27). Steadfastly refusing to yield to their requests, Margery was deserted. As Susan Dickman notes, Margery's troubles reveal a conflict over the nature of spiritual devotion. Her companions sought a social community that centered on food and fellowship. Margery sought a spiritual community that transcended the social manners of this world.[7]

Yet Margery was never able to transcend societal fear and disapproval of her life of devotion. As she grew stronger in devotion, she became more confident in her actions and more threatening to those in authority. Before she left on her first pilgrimage, her crying annoyed the villagers of Canterbury and she barely escaped trial (1.13). After she returned from Rome, her white clothes were seen as evidence of civil disobedience and she was arrested. At her trial she was questioned on her understanding of the sacraments. When she answered correctly, she was asked to defend her white clothes (1.48). She was released, only to be arrested again for her crying. After she passed a grueling examination on the articles of faith, the archbishop could not condemn her, but he called her a "very wicked woman." This inspired Margery to respond that he was a "wicked man." She was released only when she agreed to leave the area (1.62).

While her outspoken behavior certainly annoyed her critics, it is clear that Margery was never unorthodox in her beliefs. She was, however, unorthodox in her lifestyle, and this incited fear of a female uprising. The Mayor of Leicester accused her of planning to lead away the wives of the community (1.48). At her second trial the archbishop was warned that the local people had great faith in her and that she might lead them astray (1.52). Later she was brought back on charges that she counseled a noblewoman to leave her husband (1.54). Margery's recollection of their encounter was that she had advised the woman merely to love her enemies. Obviously, it was Margery's presence as a married yet independent woman that threatened the socially accepted limits of religious women. Church officials wished she would "spin and card wool, as other women do" (1.53) or enclose herself as an anchorite so that no other women could talk to her (1.13).

No matter how much she was persecuted, Margery refused to return to these accepted roles. Pilgrimage had become a way of life. Having broken out of the ordinary role of a laywoman, Margery continued to search for ways to deepen her devotion to God. She journeyed to new places to seek out God and changed her dress and eating habits many times. She was constantly on the move, physically and spiritually. She laughed at disapproval and scorn, seeing it as an opportunity to identify with the suffering of Christ (see 1.54). Like Mechthild, she did not revel in suffering, but accepted persecution as a consequence of her devotion. She saw beyond her present difficulties to the merriment that awaited her in heaven. She exhibited a reverence for spiritual ideas and an irreverence for their institutionalization.[8] Having experienced the true joy of heaven, she found all else secondary to being in the company of God.

THE SEARCH FOR OTHERS IN TEARS OF COMPASSION

However, Margery's devotion to God did not draw her out of the world. Despite the public criticism of her actions and the lack of spiritual companions, Margery remained a concerned sister and mother of the world, weeping for adversity and sin. As Hildegard suggested, there is a natural flow of love, not only between oneself and God but between oneself and the world. Having experienced the love of God, Margery asked, "Why should I not then have charity for the people and desire forgiveness of their sins?" (1.57). Having joined the company of heaven, she longed to see the company expand to encompass the whole world. The search for God led Margery to a search for others. Tears of devotion were also tears of compassion.

For Margery tears were a concrete form of Christian service. They were prayer and petition that sought not just to show compassion, but to bring compassion to others. She was told that her tears were a spiritual gift. "Blessed are you, daughter, in the weeping that you weep for people's sins, for many shall be saved thereby" (1.41). This "well of tears" for the sins of the world was active prayer on their behalf. As the confidant of God, she was able to elicit divine love through her own devotion. "You weep so every day for mercy that I have to grant it," God confessed, "and people will not believe the goodness that I work in you for them" (1.64). As a gift from God, her tears became a vehicle through which God's grace could flow to the world.

Through tears of contrition and devotion, Margery witnessed to the satisfying love of self and God. She was ordained as a mirror amongst the people, providing an example of the contrition for sin that begins the search for forgiveness and acceptance of oneself that is its reward (1.78). In her tears Margery conveyed the sorrow for sin that separates us from God and the joy that realizes the constant devotion of God. Her tears provided a model of direct access to grace that comes through experiencing the mystery of salvation. When a priest complained that she could stop her crying because Jesus was long since dead, she retorted, "Sir, his death is as fresh to me as if he had died this same day, and so, I think, it ought to be to you and to all Christian people. We ought always to remember his kindness, and always think of the doleful death that he died for us" (1.60).

Margery's own ability to keep the kindness of God fresh in her mind was a result of her ability to imagine herself as a participant in the events of salvation. The experience of salvation elicited her compassion for the pain and passion of Christ. Her role was not to imagine herself as Christ but to observe the crucifixion and mourn with those close to Christ, especially his mother, Mary. She meditated on the birth of Mary and played the role of midwife for Mary's mother, Anne. Margery spoke words of encouragement for Mary to continue in God's service. She imagined traveling with Mary to the home of Elizabeth to join in their fellowship and to assist at the birth of John the Baptist (1.6). She envisioned witnessing the birth of Jesus and continuing the journey with Mary through the flight to Egypt (1.7). While standing in the streets of Jerusalem, Margery thought about the pain and joy of Mary's farewell to her son (1.73). Like Mary, Margery longed to join Jesus in heaven, but accepted her role as comforter of Mary (1.79). At the site of the crucifixion she identified with Mary's sorrow and acted as if she were a fellow mourner (1.80). After Jesus' burial, Margery describes herself attending to Mary's grief, making a drink of gruel and wine for her (1.81). All these events, of course, were played out in Margery's imagination, but they were so real to her that a recipe for gruel is written in the margins of her book.

Through her identification with Mary, Margery took on the role of mother to Christ. As God had promised her, through weeping and mourning for Christ she became a "true mother having compassion on her child" (1.14). Sandra McEntire suggests that through her meditations Margery sought to reconcile her own feeling about being a mother.[9] In the same way that she transformed her marriage into a relationship of spiritual fellowship, she redefined her understanding of motherhood as spiritual compassion. Margery mentioned her children only once, when she counseled her son to turn away from his worldly pursuits and toward a religious life. While his initial reaction was to leave home, eventually he was transformed by her prayers on his behalf and returned to thank his mother (2.1). Her new identity as spiritual mother was confirmed by Christ, who declared that through her charity she had become a true mother to him and to all the world (1.36).

Margery's acts of charity took a variety of forms. While most people found her crying annoying, she was frequently called on to cry for others in moments of need. Sitting in vigil with the sick, she would meditate on the death of Christ and Mary and thus provide a ministry of comfort to the dying (1.72). When her home church was on fire, the townsfolk begged her to continue crying in hopes that through her compassion God would take mercy on their church. At the church door she cried, "Good Lord, make everything all right!" She writes that afterwards a snowstorm quenched the flames of the fire (1.67). Through tears of compassion she was able to minister to the world.

At other times her ministry took more active forms of service. During her pilgrimages she occasionally was called upon to act as handmaid to women in need. The most poignant example of ministry was her care for a new mother who had gone mad. When Margery spoke to her "seriously and kindly" the woman stopped her raving and was comforted. Margery prayed for her every day and continued to visit until eventually the woman was restored to health (1.75). Like Christ, who had comforted her during her madness, Margery comforted this woman and helped restore her soul.

More difficult was Margery's ministry to her husband. Having devoted herself to God and shaped a new life as mystic, pilgrim, and minister, she was called back to her home to care for her invalid husband. Her search had taken her far from home, both physically and spiritually, and it was difficult for her to go back. She realized that she would be criticized for not attending to her husband, and yet she feared that caring for him would conflict with her devotion to God. Finally she was able to reconcile her conflict by realizing that she could look after her husband for the love of God. As expected, his care distracted her from contemplation, but she saw her service as a form of devotion to God. By returning home, Margery was able to journey forward and realize the full potential of God's promise that by weeping for other people's sins and adversities, she was a true sister (1.14).

As daughter, wife, mother, and sister, Margery found satisfaction in herself, in others, and most importantly, in God. This new identity is symbolized in her description of herself as a creature. Evoking the biblical image of becoming a new creation in Christ, her journey was a concrete expression of the promise that "the old has passed away, behold, the new has come." She was reconciled to Christ and had become an ambassador for Christ in the ministry of reconciliation (2 Corinthians 5:16–21). The second half of her book gives proof of her identity as a creature of God. In 1438 she was admitted into the Trinity Guild, a group of civic leaders who governed her town. While it was logical that she be admitted by virtue of her father's prominent role in the guild, it was not until after her husband's death that she became a member. Thus she was accepted on her own terms, not as daughter of John Burnham or wife of John Kempe, but as a creature of God.

Secondly, her book ends with an example of her prayer, evidently to serve as a guide for the devotion of her readers. For those who have faith in her prayers, Margery writes, "I pray you, Lord, grant them, for the abundance of your mercy" (2.10). In noting the importance of this passage, Dhira Mahoney observes that by using the word "I," Margery is finally able to claim the search for God as her own.[10] Margery was at home at last in her awareness of herself and others through the satisfying love of God.

CONTEMPORARY REFLECTIONS

It is not easy to understand—let alone relate to—Margery's search for satisfying love. When her book was discovered and identified by Hope Allen, there was a great deal of expectation that at last scholars would have an example of medieval English piety. As Allen grew familiar with the work, she realized this was anything but a proper English mystic. Having been identified as a devout anchoress in a sixteenth-century publication, Margery had been characterized ever since as an orthodox mystic. The details of her temptations and trials changed that impression permanently. Allen herself realized that her true contemporaries were not the saintly Julian, but continental women like Bridget and Dorothea. But this assessment defied the wisdom of Allen's contemporaries and Allen died before publishing her results.[11]

With the renewed interest in medieval women mystics, scholars have taken up where Allen left off. Interpretations of Margery's life vary widely, from seeing her as a tragic example of the repressing nature of the church and society at large to praising her as the epitome of Christian humility and service. Two of the best interpreters are Ellen Ross and Clarissa Atkinson, who recognize the context of her world and yet find inspiration in the otherness of her spiritual quest. Ross suggests that we are not to find comfort in Margery's life, but to be challenged by the difference of her world and piety. Atkinson notes how Margery continues to be ordained as a mirror to challenge our assumptions about women and holiness.[12] We see in Margery's life a strange and exaggerated form of all seekers, which raises questions for us about the possibility of living a satisfied life.

It is hard to get past the impression that Margery is no more than a stereotypical crying woman. She is not a success story of satisfaction. Although she is accepted into the Trinity Guild and writes the story of her life in celebration of the event, few had the opportunity to be inspired by her life story. Only one copy of her book survived, and it was locked away in a monastery for five hundred years. When excerpts of her work were shared with the public, all but the common aspects of her life were left out. One of the most important ideas that Margery challenges is our desire to understand satisfaction as a fulfilling and respected life. When Margery talks about being "well pleased" she does not mean living a pleasing life. Her unedited life story is filled with her failures, her doubts, her struggles, her persecutions, and her attempts to grow in response to God's love. She reminds us that the atoning life is not an easy life and not a perfect life.

Margery is not a model of the satisfied life but a real example of what it costs to search for satisfaction. In search of wholeness Margery gave up the comforts of her home, her identity as wife and mother, and the respect of her community. She lived on the fringes of the church, felt forsaken by religious leaders, and was slow to trust the reality of God's love. Unlike Mechthild, who accepted the forsakenness of God as part of the freedom of love, Margery was tormented by her feelings of rejection. The realization that Margery could not please God better than by believing that she was loved is a truth that speaks to many people in our day. A colleague commented to me that she knows a woman who is just like Margery Kempe. Margery reminds us of many people caught in the spiritual dilemma of worthlessness who desire to come home to their identity in God.

One of Margery's greatest barriers to satisfaction was her shame about her sexual identity. Given our contemporary understanding of sexuality and celibacy, Margery seems anything but a whole person. The medieval context of celibacy and purity are repressive by our standards. And yet part of the struggle and the success of Margery's life is the ability to claim purity in the midst of her married state. We seek a form of physical and spiritual wholeness that was not possible in her day. Often, our idea of wholeness is having everything held together in a whole. Sexual love is an expression of, not a barrier to, love of God. Yet our era is filled with people who are tormented by the sexual mores of our day. Today homosexual Christians struggle for a definition of sexual purity in the midst of a homophobic society. Margery realized that wholeness meant making choices, searching for a sexual identity that defied the customs of her day, and preserving a sense of her self as the beloved of God.

Margery challenges us with an example of the satisfied life as an integrated life that seeks to merge awareness of herself, others, and God into a unified identity. Part of this identity is coordination of her various roles as daughter, wife, mother, and sister. She is the daughter of John Burnham and of God, the wife of John Kempe and of God, the mother of fourteen children and of Christ, the sister of a fellow mad mother and of Mary, mother of God. The challenging message of her story is that her earthly and spiritual roles do not live in conflict but build upon one another. William Provost describes Margery as bivocational, with her spiritual vocation added on to her earthly roles. Such a life was so nontypical for her day that it caused her to "struggle constantly with others and with herself over it."[13]

We may struggle most with Margery's identity as a mother to Christ. One of the central premises of Julian's theology is that motherhood is not an appropriate role for our relationship to the divine. God does not need our acts of motherly sacrifice. But Margery cannot give up her identity as a mother. Instead she weeps for Christ and shows compassion for her neighbors. At the least, Margery shows us how hard it is to overcome cultural expectations. Living in a cell, Julian could redefine God as our mother; living in the world, the best Margery could do was refocus her identity as a mother. At the most, Margery may challenge us to question our image of the self-assured and independent Christian. Is it possible that a ministry of compassion, of weeping for the suffering of the world, is an appropriate form of holiness?

The point of Margery's struggle was not to grow beyond her world but to be more fully present in it. Her journey was not about progressing toward God but about becoming more at home in God. The nonlinear structure of her book underscores the point that satisfaction is not about moving somewhere but about deepening relationships. While Mechthild sought to be in the world but not of it, Margery was of the world but not in it. She was of the Burnham family of Lynn, wife of John Kempe, and mother of fourteen children. Satisfaction was not in escaping from these roles but in refusing to be confined within them. Her efforts to redefine the meaning of daughter, wife, and mother are the essence of her search. As Elizabeth Armstrong suggests, Margery does not seek to find herself in heaven's realm, but to find God in hers.[14]

One of the most important ways that Margery finds God in her realm is through conversations with other like-minded souls. The support of advisers such as Julian and the heavenly companionship of Jesus and Mary are moments of confirmation and grace. Although Margery is faithful in her attendance at mass and penance, she rarely finds God in the usual sacraments of the church. This should be a warning for those of us in the church today. If we listen to the seekers of our day, we too may realize that our ministry of Word and sacrament offers little of the saving grace of God. Margery experienced the Word in the words of encouragement, discernment, and even criticism of others. Her experience is of a God in relation to the world, in relation to her life as daughter, sister, and mother. Ultimately, it is the experience of herself as creature related to the Creator of the world.

Finding our Creator is the essence of Julian's message of satisfying love. We are trapped by our worldly assessment of our failures, but Christ comes into the world to preach the message of God's accepting love. To see the world through God's eyes is a difficult task and requires the cultivation of Christ to wear away the internalization of societal standards and to heal, revive, and restore the soul. For Margery it required a spiritual awakening, years of divine assurance, and the continuing support of church leaders. To catch a vision of heaven draws us toward a new relationship with God that longs for satisfaction. The suffering of such love, as Mechthild writes, is a paradox of the beauty and yet limitation of our ability to love God. It brought Margery to the heights of devotion and caused her to sorrow for the sin present in herself and others that blocked her vision of heaven. Caught by such a vision, we are called out of ourselves into a vision of the whole world revived and restored in God. As Hildegard saw, working for the coming of this realm becomes the focus of life, engaging us in satisfying work. In Margery we see that work provide ministry and comfort for those in her world.

Margery could not have read the works of Julian, Mechthild, and Hildegard, but her life has much in common with their visions of atonement. It provides a challenging example for us of the possibilities and costs of searching for an atoning life.

✼ ✼ ✼

chapter six

HADEWIJCH OF BRABANT ON
SERVICE IN
THE SATISFIED LIFE

Margery Kempe provides one model of the satisfied life as a life of searching. But it is not the only example of satisfaction. Just as there have been a variety of theologies of atonement through the ages; there are a variety of models of the atoned life. As Hildegard observed, it is virtue that satisfies, for it is in our work on behalf of the coming of God's realm of justice that we touch God. For Margery Kempe service was a by-product of searching for satisfaction. But can service be satisfying in and of itself? Can service be the vehicle by which we become at one with God?

The idea of Christian service has been heralded through the ages as the model of the Christian life. In our own day the most widely acclaimed Christian, Mother Teresa, was known for her service to the poor. Churches depend on the service of volunteers to do everything from teaching the faith to ministering to the community. The ability to realize the potential of the realm of God depends on the service of those dedicated to work for the coming of God's justice in the world. In order to maintain the ongoing work of the church, there is a growing need for people to accept the call to full-time service in ministry. In society as a whole, service professions are a growth industry because of the ever expanding needs of our growing and aging population.

Many Christians, especially women, respond to the need for servants only to discover that service is anything but satisfying. Servants are overworked, underpaid, and rarely appreciated. This is particularly true in the church. Too often, those who serve are overwhelmed with demands for more service. Frustration is met with the command to take up one's cross and follow Jesus. Failure, disrespect, and guilt lead to burnout. The experience of service is not one of touching God, but of touching the limitations of our abilities and our communities.

If Hildegard is correct in saying it is virtue that satisfies, we will have to rethink the meaning of Christian service. Hildegard herself, however, provides more of a model of leadership than of service, since she was primarily an abbess, prophet, preacher, and writer. A better corollary to our idea of service is the lifestyle of those known as the social workers of the Middle Ages, the beguines. Mechthild was a beguine, but her writing focused on the experience of God rather than the experience of service. It is another beguine, Hadewijch of Brabant, who gives us the best insight into the beguine life.

A younger contemporary of Mechthild, Hadewijch both lived as a beguine and headed a beguine community. She lived in an area that was very accepting of beguines, at a time when beguines were relatively free from church counsel or censure. Beguines lived a semireligious life devoted to God but free from permanent vows of poverty, chastity, and obedience. In 1215 Jacques de Vitry received approval from the pope for the establishment of beguine communities. At this time beguines often lived together in informal communities with a mistress who directed their activities and spiritual progress. They earned their own living through various trades, followed a schedule of prayers and meditations, and served the poor and outcast in hospitals, schools, and orphanages. Hadewijch was evidently one of these mistresses, and most of her writing was for the instruction of the beguines under her charge. Her letters hint at some controversy over her leadership and suggest she was separated and exiled from the community. Since we have no further writing or record of her life, it is inferred that she retired to a hospital or orphanage to live until her death.

Unlike the narrative style of Margery's writing, Hadewijch's writing is in the form of letters, visions, and poetry. Most of the letters are written for a beloved beguine, instructing her on the ideal life. They read like an advice column on beguine life. They also contain moments of self-reflection that show the struggle and frustration of Hadewijch's life. The visions are even more self-revealing. They give an account of her mystical experiences, establish her spiritual authority, and provide models for the contemplation of her community. While the contents of her visions are far-fetched for contemporary readers, they give us insight into the spiritual practice that undergirds the beguine life. Inserted in the visions is a list of perfect Christians who were meant to serve as models of faith for the beguines. It is from this list that we can determine the time frame for her writing to be approximately 1220–1240. (It is interesting to note that Hildegard of Bingen is included as one of the perfect.) Yet it is the poetry that is often heralded as her greatest work because of its use of courtly love imagery. While the poetry is admired today for its form, the original intent was to serve as a rallying cry to service. Hildegard's pictures help one to see the nature of the world; Hadewijch's poetry inspires one to do work in the world. Her poetry was meant to elicit desire more than to illuminate the mind.

Like Mechthild's, Hadewijch's poetry was written in the form of love mysticism grounded in the themes of courtly love. Paul Mommaers has called Hadewijch the most important exponent of love mysticism.[1] Hadewijch used the ideas of the love of a knight and lady, but she typically cast God as Lady Love and the soul as the knight. This gender reversal differs from the works of the majority of love mystics, including Mechthild, who described the soul as the lady and God as the knight or lord. It provided the opportunity to focus on the active role of the soul serving "his" Lady in love. Elizabeth Wainwright-deKadt observes that Hadewijch used the form of courtly poetry because it spoke of the ideals of love for a group. Hadewijch was, therefore, trying to create a group of people she could talk to on her own level.[2] Hadewijch used courtly love imagery to create a community that she could talk to about service.

Her visions balanced this depiction of the ideal of love with the reality of her experience of love. Scholars are beginning to see the significance of her visions, and certainly in her own day the visions would have spoken more directly than the poems of the life of serving Love. The visions contain few details outside the visionary experience and are arranged thematically rather than chronologically. The first vision is often cited as the most important, providing a summary of her life. Having received communion, Hadewijch envisioned being lifted spiritually into a meadow filled with trees. Her first discovery was the tree of human nature, with a solid trunk that represented the soul, a rotten root that symbolized the "brittle nature" of humanity, and a frail but beautiful flower that represented the human shape. She was led further through the forest past the tree of humility, the tree of perfect will, and the tree of discernment, and finally arrived at the tree of wisdom. Commenting on the symbolism of the three branches of wisdom, Hadewijch wrote, "For to carry Love means a propensity, a longing, a desire, a service, an incessant exercise of burning will. But to feel Love means the awareness of being in the liberty of Love. But to be Love surpasses all" (*V*, 1.138).[3] Having understood the tree of wisdom, Hadewijch saw an uprooted tree that she was instructed to climb all the way to the roots of God. She was sent off on her journey with the blessing, "Give all, for all is yours!" (*L*, 1.408).

These three themes of carrying Love, feeling Love, and being Love are repeated several times throughout her writing. In letter six, Hadewijch describes the beguine life as a life of noble service and suffering exile that lead to God's touching the soul (*L*, 6.361). The same three themes are repeated in letter twenty-three, when Hadewijch advises that if God is yours in Love, you must live for God by yourself being Love (*L*, 23.2). To serve Love is to carry Love, be in Love's noble service, to live for God. To serve Love is to feel Love, to suffer in exile for Love, to realize that God is yours. To serve Love is to be Love, to grow up in Love, to be God with God. It is as we further explore these themes that we see how the life of service satisfied Hadewijch.

CARRYING LOVE IN NOBLE SERVICE

For Hadewijch serving Love was honorable work. Its heart is the law of chivalry, in which service is the worthy and noble pursuit of Love. "The only rest of such a heart is to do its utmost for the sake of its Beloved and to render him love and honor in view of his sublimity; and to offer him noble service as a gift—not for pay in the hand, but because Love herself at all times is satisfaction and pay enough" (*L*, 12.53). In another letter Hadewijch urges her beguines to serve Love worthily by prevailing in service and specifically mentions reciting the hours of prayer and keeping the rule of beguine life as two aspects of service (*L*, 2.66). Elizabeth Dreyer notes that Hadewijch saw service as an undying call to be ever ready to respond to the call and needs of Love. "For Hadewijch, the call to serve Love is the whole point of being involved with God."[4]

To convey the identity of this noble service, Hadewijch envisions the soul as the knight of Love. The soul is the warrior for Love, engaging in great combat for Love, enduring fierce assault, and laying siege for Love (see *PS*,

2.1; *PS*, 8.6; *L*, 18.13). Hadewijch's poetry is filled with these themes. Like the knight who labors to win his lady, Hadewijch serves to capture Love. "He who wishes to serve Love alone," she writes, "with all his heart and all his powers, has wisely laid out the whole siege, so that he may wholly capture Love" (*PS*, 8.6). Hadewijch describes this service as like a jousting match in which a knight competes to prove his love (see *PC*, 1:79–88; *PS*, 32:7). Such a knight is clothed in the fine garments and fine language of a true noble, performing acts with ardor, never being self-complacent, and always having regard for the needs of strangers (*PS*, 9:4). For Hadewijch, to take on this noble-mindedness (see *L*, 6.191) is to make herself and her beguines active agents in service.

Yet Hadewijch is careful to distinguish the call to serve from the necessity to succeed in service. Be compassionate to sinners, she advises, "but do not take on yourself to keep reciting prayers for them or earnestly wish that God withdraw them from that state; for you would waste your time, and in other respects it would not be of much use" (*L*, 6.54). At another point she scolds a beguine for wasting her time in too many activities and urges her to observe moderation (*L*, 5.37). She counsels her charges to do good work for the honor of Love with no care for profit or for salvation. She recommends that they be docile and prompt to those in need, joyful or mournful as appropriate, devoted to the sick, generous to the poor, but satisfy everyone only "as far as you can manage it without debasing yourself." The goal, she writes, is to be "recollected in spirit beyond the reach of all creatures" (*L*, 2.14). Throughout her letters Hadewijch stresses a sense of personal agency and noble dignity that does not sacrifice self for the sake of service.

In order to keep the proper perspective on service, Hadewijch suggests that one prepare for it as for a pilgrimage. First, one needs to follow the right path, which is the way of Jesus, the saints, and devout company. Along the way one must beware of the thieves of temptation and the vice of self-satisfaction. As one experiences pains, one should bend forward to endure them, but walk erect in fulfilling one's own needs as well as the needs of others. Finally, one should seek support from others through prayers of the people and the love of God (*L*, 15.104). Like the knight that embarks on a quest for his beloved, the beguine must think of herself as a pilgrim focused on service to Love.

Hadewijch's expectation is that the quest will be rewarded, either through winning Love or receiving a reward from her Lord. Hadewijch describes Love as a rich fief, meaning that the reward for service is the love that one receives (*PC*, 16.55–58). At other points she talks about the compensation due from the knight's lord. If the knight faithfully serves Love, he must be paid "measure for measure" so that his whole life becomes divinized (*PC*, 14.148–162). Behind this idea of reward is not the typical idea of merit but the idea of obligation that binds feudal service. The two-way relationship of lord to knight was one of protection and support in return for service. This mutual relationship was understood to provide for the knight as well as serve the lord. Christians are obligated to service, Hadewijch writes, out of homage to the "incomparable sublimity of God, who created our nature to this end" (*L*, 6.316). To see God in this role of Lord emphasizes a mutual relationship in which God could appropriately demand service and the beguines could demand protection and favors.[5]

Ulrike Wiethaus suggests that for Hadewijch good works are ritual acts that bring the individual closer to the ideal of being created in the image of God.[6] Like Julian and Mechthild, Hadewijch stresses the goodness of our creation in the image of God. In her first vision she saw the human soul as a strong trunk that blooms into the beautiful flower of the human shape. Later in this same vision Christ commanded her to stand up, "entirely free and without fall" (*V*, 1.265). In another vision Hadewijch proclaims that by making her perfect, God had taken all her lowness away (*V*, 4.56). Thus the obligation to serve is based in the ability to act upon the grace-given condition of creation. Like Hildegard, Hadewijch describes this work as cultivating the field of our soul (*L*, 10.83, 93).

It is in the context of this confidence in the goodness of our creation that Hadewijch urges her charges not only to strive for divinity but to model the humanity of God. Here Hadewijch talks about carrying Love as carrying the cross. "God knows there are few of us who want to live as men [*sic*] with his Humanity, or want to carry his cross with him, or want to hang on the cross with him and pay humanity's debt to the full" (*L*, 6.227). The nature of this debt is described in letter thirty as a debt of unity. The Trinity is created in unity and humanity is created in the image of this unity. Failing to "answer the demand" of unity, humanity fell. Christ was born to satisfy this debt and died and rose and ascended to complete the unity of God. "So it is also with us," Hadewijch writes, "when payment of the debt we owe is demanded of us by the Trinity, grace is given us to live worthily according to the noble Trinity, as is fitting." Service is fitting, because it is the obligation due one's Lord and it is modeled in the life of Christ. But it is also an obligation that can demand reciprocation. "We are now under Love's demand toward the

Holy Trinity. Therefore we ourselves must make a demand on Love, and we must do this with all ardor; and we must demand nothing else but his [sic] Unity" (*L*, 30.57, 68, 84).

Hadewijch links her understanding of noble service not only with the idea of carrying the cross of the humanity of God, but of being carried by the love of God in unity with us. Love brings God down to us (*L*, 12.53). Unlike Anselm, who sees satisfaction solely in the context of the master and servant relationship, Hadewijch understands satisfaction in the midst of our noble obligation of service and our courtly relationship to Love. The identity of Love in Hadewijch's writings is debated amongst scholars, but is best understood not only as a Being who is a Lady and Queen, and an experience of love, but as the bearer of God to humanity.[7] It is Love that redeems us, and it is in the noble service of Love that we are carried to the unity of God. Love is Christ, and Christ is Love. That is why Hadewijch is able to say that "Love herself at all times is satisfaction" (*L*, 12.53). Created in the image of the Trinity's unity, we are called to return to this unity in Love.

FEELING LOVE IN SUFFERING EXILE

Hadewijch's description of noble service has much in common with Hildegard's concept of virtue. Service is enabled by the goodness of creation. The Fall is conceived as a lack of response to this creation. Christ restores the justice or the unity of the universe and makes it possible for humans to engage in virtue or service. Noble service is the greening of the soul. But for Hadewijch service is understood within the context of the relationship of courtly love. Like Mechthild, Hadewijch sees that love is both noble and suffering. It celebrates the mutuality of relationship with God but also realizes the longing and lack of control inherent between lovers. Thus, while Hildegard and Hadewijch both see that it is in service that we experience God, Hadewijch confesses the pain and anxiety of that touch. Her idea of service, then, "is mingled with a more subjective element: associated with desire, this novelty of love reveals the infinite dimensions of spiritual life; at the same time, there is suffering delving always deeper and an urge to penetrate into a mystery becoming more and more profound."[8] It is this subjectivity of love that gives us insight into the spirituality that undergirds Hadewijch's desire for service.

In letter eleven, Hadewijch gives us a rare glimpse into her feeling of love. While the purpose of the letter is to encourage a beguine to greater love of God, Hadewijch quickly turns to a description of her own feeling of love. Since she was ten years old, she writes, she was overwhelmed by the intense love of God. It is a love that she describes as being like the custom of friends, with a close feeling that relishes, devours, drinks, and swallows each other. It is a love that contents her and, she believes, contents God. It is such a unique love that Hadewijch confesses that she feels no one loves God as intensely as she. She admits that reasonably this is not possible, but she has a hard time believing it. In fact she cannot endure the thought that anyone could love God more. Finally she states that she does not believe there is anyone living by whom God is loved so much (L, 11.10).

At first glance this confession of Hadewijch's jealous love seems an unusual way to inspire devotion in another. The repetition of the idea that she loves God best hints at an arrogance and pride that is contrary to Christian virtue. In fact, in other letters Hadewijch affirms the virtue of pride. In letter eighteen she writes, "Veritable Love never had the restrictions of matter, but is free in the rich liberty of God, always giving in richness, and working with pride, and growing in nobleness" (L, 19.27). God works with pride because it is a desire to grow in love and therefore grow in noble service. It reveals an "erotic desire which has to be sublimated into an enduring 'servitude' to the ideal of Love."[9]

The means of this sublimation is humility, which Hadewijch defines as the power to receive Love. This form of humility is first found in Mary, who tames Love in the incarnation and thus discloses Love to us. No one could understand Love, she writes, "until Mary, in her flawlessness, with deep humility, had received Love. Love first was wild and then was tame; Mary gave us for the Lion a Lamb. She illuminated the darkness that had been somber for long ages" (PS, 29.4). Here it is Mary that takes on the role of effecting redemption, and humility is the means for reconciling humanity and God.

In another poem Hadewijch describes humility as the strongest of all things because it can "conquer the power of great Love." Again Mary is the model of this humility, which made the Lord so submissive that he fell "from his sublimity into this unfathomable chasm" (PC, 2.61–70). Hadewijch heralds Mary as the model of true womanhood and humility as woman's true strength. She advises her beguines to embrace this image of womanhood by being humble and noble: "Then your hearts will become wide and deep; then shall come to you that conduit which flowed to Mary without measure" (PS,

29.12). Through humility beguines are able to gain access to the love that is their strength and source of true pride.

The feeling of love not only couples pride and humility but balances love and reason. Hadewijch's torment is caused, in part, by the conflict of reason and love. Reason tells her she cannot be the most loved by God, yet she does not feel it is true. The conflict of the two constitutes the total feeling of love so that they work hand in hand to strengthen her desire to serve. In letter eighteen Hadewijch explains that reason instructs love and love enlightens reason so that they are of "great mutual help one to the other." Reason sees what God is not, thus holding love within bounds; and love sees what God is, thus propelling reason to abandon itself in love (L, 18.80). In a vision Hadewijch sees Reason as a queen adorned in an eye-covered dress. This queen commands Hadewijch to acknowledge her own reason. When Hadewijch submits, Reason becomes subject to her and Love embraces her (V, 9.40). By seeing Reason as a female figure, Hadewijch is able to acknowledge her own power of reason.

The power of reason is crucial for Hadewijch because it helps her to discern truthfully her ability to love. "It is important not just to love, but to know what one loves and, in fact, that one truly loves, and is not just in love with one's own feelings."[10] Hadewijch names this ability to discern the truth of love "noble unfaith." "So high is unfaith that it continually fears either that it does not love enough, or that it is not enough loved" (L, 8.27). Hadewijch urges her beguines to embrace these fears because they enlarge one's consciousness and increase desire. Rather than responding in anger, one must wait alone in the hope of possessing Love. In another letter Hadewijch writes that this way of despair leads one "very deep into God . . . above all the ramparts and through all the passageways, and into all places where the truth is" (L, 22.169). John Giles Milhaven notes that unfaith keeps Hadewijch from being satisfied with anything less than the full possession of God's love.[11] The knowledge that she cannot love God the best keeps her serving in search of more from Love.

These moments of despair create a deep longing that Hadewijch calls the madness of love. In the prelude to one of her most profound visions, Hadewijch describes her own experience of madness: "My heart and my veins and all my limbs trembled and quivered with eager desire and, as often occurred with me, such madness and fear beset my mind that it seemed to me I did not content my Beloved, and that my Beloved did not fulfill my desire, so that dying I must go mad, and going mad I must die" (V, 7.1). Such longing propels Hadewijch to understand and taste God to the full; nothing less could satisfy her desire. In her poems she describes this longing as a hunger for Love. May new assault of Love create a hunger so vast, Hadewijch writes, "that new Love may devour new eternity!" (*PS*, 33.14). Such souls "burn with inextinguishable fire" with mouths open, arms outstretched, and hearts open to God (*L*, 22.201, 183).

This hungering and burning madness are, like unfaith and reason, means to a deeper feeling of love. It is the longing that realizes the freedom of the Beloved. To find satisfaction in serving Love she must desire more from herself and from her Beloved. At one point Hadewijch describes this mad desire as a "rich fief" because it can unite opposites, making bitter the sweetness of love. Like reason, it propels one into deeper levels of love. "Anyone who recognized this," Hadewijch observes, "would not ask Love for anything else" (*PS*, 28.4).

Like Mechthild, Hadewijch realizes that to serve Love is to suffer in exile. Although Hadewijch lived in a time and place that welcomed beguines, she still encountered opposition and estrangement. Her letters hint at jealousy among her community and opposition to her leadership. She laments the "false brethren" who seek to interfere and destroy her community (*L*, 5.13; also see *L*, 23.11; *L*, 12.139). Hadewijch herself seems to be under special attack, perhaps because of her constant urging to accept nothing less than service to the fullness of Love. In letter twenty-five Hadewijch mentions specifically a beguine named Sara who has evidently rejected Hadewijch's leadership. While scolding her for her lack of desire for Love, Hadewijch confesses that she is wounded by Sara's betrayal. Having been forgotten by Sara, Hadewijch is left "in the lurch" (*L*, 25.2). In her next letter she notes that she must now wander alone (*L*, 26.24), exiled from Love and exiled from her community.

There is no record of the nature of her exile or the final conclusion of her conflicts. She provides few details because her letters are written to someone who is fully aware of her disgrace. One of Hadewijch's last letters is written to console and comfort this beguine. Hadewijch urges her not to grieve on Hadewijch's behalf. "What happens to me, whether I am wandering in the country or put in prison—however it turns out, it is the work of Love" (*L* 29.1). Her confidence is based on the fact that she has served the community nobly. In love she has attended to the needs of her community, dealt mercifully with their sins, and judged justly in unity with the truth of God. Yet she notes that these very actions led those alien to feeling Love to abhor her. "I remain a human being," she confesses, "who must suffer to the death with Christ in Love; for whoever lives in veritable Love will suffer opprobrium from all aliens" (L, 29.85). Those who feel Love will always suffer ridicule and contempt from the world.

Hadewijch's confidence in the midst of her exile comes from having felt the divine touch of satisfaction. Like many beguines, her highest moments of feeling Love are experienced during communion. After receiving the bread and wine, she envisions Christ as a man who took her in his arms. He "pressed me to him," she writes, "and all my members felt his in full felicity, in accordance with the desire of my heart and my humanity" (V, 7.64). It was an experience, Hadewijch observes, in which she could see, taste, and feel Love. It is a description of love that rivals Mechthild for its erotic intensity. Hadewijch calls Divine Touch the highest gift of Love. Having cherished Love with humility, led it with reason, and vanquished Love with faithfulness in suffering, she is called fully to taste Love (V, 13.179, 228). Through pride, humility, unfaith, madness, and exile, Hadewijch is truly able to feel Love.

The touch of Love helps Hadewijch not only to endure, but to leave the sufferings and failures of her service behind. Like a knight who endures all for the sake of Love, Hadewijch knows that her sufferings are no obstacle to the feel of Love. She finds comfort in the courtliness of love with its promise of reward for service. "For the Beloved is courtly and understands courtliness in love," she writes. The pains and exile paid in service to Love only increase the reward, for Love cannot fail "to mete out the same measure of love" in return. The goal is not to endure suffering but to feel Love. Once touched by Love, one forgets all memory of suffering in exile. "As long as we serve in order to attain Love, we must attend to this service. But when we love the Beloved with love, we must exclude all the rest and have fruition of Love" (L, 21.21–40). Service is the vehicle by which one feels Love, not the end. Like Mary, those who suffer in humble service to Love can conquer anything, even Love itself. And it is in this knowledge that even service in exile can be satisfying.

BEING GOD IN GROWN-UP LOVE

Through noble service and humble suffering Hadewijch is able to reach the fullness of Love. "For that is the most perfect satisfaction," she writes, "To grow up in order to be God with God" (V, 7.1). Her own experience of perfect satisfaction is recorded in vision thirteen, in which Hadewijch proclaims that Love is made fully known to her. Hadewijch imagines herself led by Mary to the depths of love, where she is instructed to join the company of those few who are full-grown in Love. She neither sees a lord nor feels his touch, but sinks into the abyss of God. The experience is too intense for words, but Hadewijch describes the effects: "I knew and beheld all things, and in it I saw height, amplitude, and depth. Then fruition overcame me as before, and I sank into the fathomless depth and came out of the spirit in that hour, of which one can never speak at all" (V, 13.228, 252). To rest in God is to enter into the abyss of God and be God.

To proclaim that one can be God is the completion of the divinization promised to the knight that contents Love. A strange concept to us, this fullness of union with God is a constant theme in Christian mysticism. To be created in the image of God, or as Hadewijch would say, with a solid trunk, is to be given the possibility of growing to the fullness of our image in God. Hadewijch experiences this fullness as full-grown Love. It is the fulfillment of traveling to the root of God promised in her first vision. Wiethaus calls this experience of abyss "a divine epiphany of God/ess as the whirlpool/womb of all life."[12] As she rests in the height, amplitude, and depth of love, she no longer carries or feels Love; she is Love.

It is this fullness of Love that gives Hadewijch the self-confidence that so pervades her letters and poetry. Like the knight who completes his quest and returns home to glory, Hadewijch's love grows to be home with God. The one who travels the roads to the land of high Love, Hadewijch writes, "will find his beloved and his country at the end" (PS, 9.3). It is a country of wholeness in which all the paradoxes of carrying and feeling Love are joined. It is out of this fullness that Hadewijch writes, "I have integrated all my diversity, and I have individualized all my wholeness. And I have enclosed all my individuality in God" (L, 28.242). Don Nugent suggests that in Hadewijch we find a "harvest of wholeness."[13] It is a wholeness that finds Hadewijch at home with herself in God.

The result of this wholeness is an empowering flow of love between the soul and God. In letter nine Hadewijch writes that the loved and the Beloved so abide in one another that "one sweet *divine Nature* flows through them both" (L, 9.4). The flow is a two-way exchange, which Hadewijch describes as a passageway of freedom: "God is a way for the passage of the soul into its liberty, that is, into his inmost depths, which cannot be touched except by the soul's abyss" (L, 18.63). In one of her poems Hadewijch names this flow of love as a living spring that is beyond comprehension. "This flowing forth and this reflux of one into the other, and this growth in God, surpass the mind and understanding, the intelligence and capacity of human creatures" (*PC*, 16.129–133).

It is in the context of her understanding of full-grown Love that Hadewijch returns to the imagery of courtly love to describe the relationship between the soul and God as one of competing knights. Not only does she see God as Lady Love and her Lord, but as a fellow knight engaged in battle. Love is a mean fighter, able to deliver heavy blows and to inflict wounds "from which no one can recover." She is also a crafty fighter, fencing under the shield, which is considered an illegal move in war etiquette (*PS*, 39.6). In response Hadewijch urges her beguines to fight back. "We must continually dare to fight her in new assaults with all our strength, all our knowledge, all our wealth, all our love, all these alike. This is how to behave with the Beloved" (*L*, 7.4). Hadewijch suggests fighting Love with longing (*PS*, 38.7) and with passion. She counsels the "valiant lover" who dares to fight Love not to give way, but to catch hold of Love, striking before she strikes (*PS*, 39.10).

This fighting against Love is, for Hadewijch, an expression of the freedom of love. The one who has never fought against Love "has never lived a free day" (*PS*, 21.5). To serve Love is to refuse to be servile to one's neighbors and to God. In the full growth of Love, the soul both conquers and is conquered by Love. "The noble soul in Love's service lives so free that it dares to fight her with passion to the death, or nearly, until it conquers the power of Love" (*PS*, 40.3). To be free is to have the power of Love. It is to be free with God and in God. Such freedom empowers Hadewijch to remain free from the criticism of her community and free from settling for anything less than the full depth of being Love.

Hadewijch calls those grown up in Love "champions" (*PS*, 40.4). Having carried Love in fulfillment of their obligation of service and left the obligation behind in feeling Love, they are fully satisfied in the transformation into Love. The fullest satisfaction is to live Love. "Love alone," she advises, "is the thing that can satisfy us" (*L*, 7.4). It is a satisfaction that propels Hadewijch into the world to serve Love. "For my part," Hadewijch concludes, "I am devoted to these works at any hour and still perform them at all times, to seek after nothing but Love, work nothing but Love, protect nothing but Love, and advance nothing but Love" (*L*, 17.123). As Milhaven notes, "It is in freedom with another that one satisfies one's desire."[14] It is in the freedom of being Love that Hadewijch finds herself and God and satisfaction in a life of service.

CONTEMPORARY REFLECTIONS

Hadewijch is not a model of satisfaction for the average person. Even in her own time John of Leeuwen heralded Hadewijch as a glorious woman who was an authentic spiritual guide, but useful only to those "opened by pure and silent love."[15] Even today she is described as professing an "extraordinarily assertive and aggressive form of mysticism" that refused "anything less than everything for herself and demanded the same of others."[16] Her demand to live a full-grown Love stretched herself and her community to the limit of their abilities. Many, not able to endure the pilgrimage she envisioned, forsook her goal of service.

Hadewijch is an example of an elite form of Christian life meant for the few who dare to find satisfaction in service. Unlike Margery, who expresses the more common experience of searching for the love of God, Hadewijch provides a model of a confident woman who not only found God's love but dared to be God in love. She was a woman who wrote for women in an era of rising opportunity for women. Mother Columba Hart, who translated Hadewijch's writings into English, suggests that Hadewijch has a particular appeal for modern women, enabling them to escape from their cultural oppression and find hope in the idea of growing in love.[17] With the growing opportunities for women today, Hadewijch sets a precedent for a self-assertive yet committed style of Christian service.

The courtly images that she used to describe her life may not have modern appeal. Few women today resonate with the idea of being a knight in God's service. Yet for Hadewijch this image symbolized a form of active love that far surpassed the traditional image of lover mysticism. As a knight she could engage in noble service, actively show her devotion to Lady Love, and know that she would be protected and rewarded by her Lady's Lord. She could also imagine herself as an agent of love able to fight for Love's attention and to fight Love in freedom. Elizabeth Petroff observes that Hadewijch represents a new kind of feminine spirit "in which desire and satisfaction cannot be distinguished, just as masculine and feminine cannot be distinguished." The effect is to empower herself and the beguines under her care to be capable of "anything and all things."[18]

This merging of gender imagery is one of the most intriguing aspects of Hadewijch's understanding of service. As a part of this new feminine spirit, Hadewijch transforms the image of the Christian woman. Nowhere in her writing do we find the sense of forsakenness and self-negation that is typical of woman mystics. Her madness is not the despair and self-doubt that plagued Margery. Hadewijch advocates pride as a virtue, embraces unfaith and madness as agents of increased desire, envisions Reason as a female figure, and transforms humility from a sign of weakness to women's greatest strength. The model of true womanhood, Mary, is able to summon Christ and tame Love through the depth of her own love, which becomes a conduit to the Love of God. The masculine traits of pride and reason— along with the feminine traits of madness, humility, and unfaith—are transformed as aspects of an integrated female identity of wholeness.

Likewise, Hadewijch mixes masculine and feminine images of Christ. Christ is the exemplar of suffering in exile. His loving service is a means for satisfying the debt to the unity of the Trinity. Hadewijch is challenged to the same level of suffering and sees her service as the debt she owes to the unity of God. Here Hadewijch comes close to the form of self-sacrificial love that can entrap rather than embody satisfaction. When she writes that Christ is born to satisfy our debt, her theology has more in common with that of Anselm than of Julian. But she avoids the dangers of a traditional understanding of satisfactionary atonement by coupling this understanding of Christ as suffering servant with an interpretation of Christ as Lady Love. Here Hadewijch is one not only with Christ's humanity but with his divinity, which fills her with the height, depth, and fullness of God. In full-grown love to Love she is not a servant or a mistress but a partner with Christ fighting with him and against him in the freedom of Love. This is why, in the end, her true identity is as a knight, not a mere servant of God.

Hadewijch's life of serving Love combines Mechthild's ideas of longing for satisfaction and Hildegard's confidence in satisfying work with Julian's insight that satisfaction is an affair of love. For Julian and Hadewijch the love of God is based in courtesy toward humanity, which reaches out in protection and care. Both talk about the honorable nature of God and the reward of salvation offered to humanity. Mechthild adds to this understanding of courtesy the longing and freedom of Love, which challenges the soul to endure suffering exile. Hadewijch uses many of the same ideas, but by imagining the soul as knight rather than mistress of Love, she displays a pride and confidence in her quest that eludes Mechthild. Thus, Hadewijch experiences a wholeness in love that is similar to the conception of wholeness found in Hildegard. The flow of light that illumines Hildegard's vision is the flow of Love that characterizes being God with God for Hadewijch. While Hadewijch never clarifies what the unity is that the Trinity demands, Christ accomplishes, and we are to emulate, it is possible to understand it in light of the realm of justice that Hildegard envisions at the beginning and end of creation.

It is this unique understanding of herself as the knight of Love, in service to Love and empowered by Love, that makes Hadewijch an intriguing model of the satisfied life. She is able to embody the totality of her desire, including madness and despair, while Margery struggles against them. That is why Hadewijch is able to embrace the idea of humble service that so challenges Margery. While Margery endures service, especially the care of her husband, as an expression of devotion to Christ, Hadewijch revels in service, because in it she lives the Love of God.

In comparing their lives, we see that the historical circumstances influence their experience of satisfaction. While both strove to create a new form of relationship to God, Margery lived in a culture more fearful of innovation and more restrictive of women's roles than that of Hadewijch. Likewise, the forms of lay piety in Margery's culture were less innovative. The love mysticism that was popular in Hadewijch's day had been replaced by affective piety in Margery's day. Once again, women's lives do not necessarily progress in history. Too, the models of Christian life that will resonate to contemporary women will depend on the circumstances of their lives. For those struggling with cultural restrictions placed on women, Margery provides a model of searching for satisfaction. For those privileged to live in a time and place that provide new freedom for women, Hadewijch's vision of service is a challenging model of the satisfied life.

I see Hadewijch-like devotion to service among a select group of young people who are passionate about their love for God. They are often impatient with feminist theology and do not understand the need for inclusive language. Their theology is not built on the experience of women's oppression, but on an inherent sense of their self-worth. They freely embrace the masculine and feminine aspects of their identity and resonate with cartoon figures like Xena the warrior princess, who is dressed to accentuate her female body, but fights evil with manly courage. In them I see the kind of pride that will settle for nothing less than the most out of themselves and a kind of spiritual humility that dares to tame God. As I look at them, I realize that the world in which they live is filled with opportunities that were unheard of, even in my time. Hadewijch is a model of satisfaction for this new generation.

✷ ✷ ✷

chapter seven

CATHERINE OF SIENA ON
SUFFERING OF
THE SATISFIED LIFE

We can understand the Christian life as searching for satisfying love and even consider the
possibility that service may be a means
toward satisfaction, but is there satisfaction
in suffering? To ask such a question is important for two reasons. First of all, current
research has argued that for many medieval
women suffering was understood as meaningful, not just as a consequence of
Christian faith, but as the center of the Christian life. Caroline Bynum makes
the provocative suggestion that "we should not turn our backs so resolutely as
we have recently done either on the possibility that suffering can be fruitful
or on food and female body as positive, complex, resonant symbols of love
and generosity."[1] But what would it mean to consider suffering as fruitful?
Entertaining such a question will challenge many of the insights of this study;
namely that self-sacrifice is what we need to be atoned from, not the vehicle
by which we become reconciled to God. Considering a model of the satisfied
life so foreign to our time and so outside the normal rhetoric of feminist theology has the possibility of drawing us out of our presuppositions about satisfaction and clarifying the true meaning of the satisfied life. Such an approach
suggests a confidence that, even in their otherness, medieval women provide
insight for theological reflection.

A second reason to consider suffering as a possible model of Christian life is that suffering is real, both in the life of Jesus and our lives. By refusing to see any salvific significance in Jesus' suffering, feminist theologians have been unable to articulate how God overcomes suffering. As Darby Ray notes, the problem with feminist theology is that it cannot articulate any divine "redemptive response to evil."[2] The best one can do is to say that God feels our suffering, which leaves us in the position of having to overcome evil. Once again we return to the trap of having to save ourselves. As a result, the experience of suffering is bracketed as outside the realm of the saving work of God. Feminist theology denounces self-sacrifice as a way to understand suffering, but is silent on how we can understand suffering in the life of satisfaction.

Both to explore the full range of medieval models of satisfaction and to address the silence of feminist theology on the meaning of suffering, we turn to one of the most celebrated and controversial women of the Middle Ages, Catherine of Siena. Catherine is one of the most famous Christians of all time, declared both a saint and a doctor of theology by the Roman Catholic Church, meaning that both her life and her teaching are considered outstanding models of Christian faith. This assessment is, in part, a result of the way she responded to the remarkable evils of her day. She lived in the fourteenth century, a time of turmoil in her city, the church, and her religious order. The center of this controversy was the erosion of the power of the papacy. Born during the period of the Avignon papacy, when the center of the church had been moved from Italy to France, Catherine worked to return the pope to Rome, only to see him die and the church split over the naming of his successor. Her life of sanctity was a stark contrast to the feuding, political positioning, and warfare of church leaders.

Instability in the church inflamed family rivalries and political alliances. The plague, which hit Siena three times during Catherine's lifetime, intensified social unrest even more. Surrounded by suffering of all kinds, she responded as best she could by mediating family feuds and treating the sick. Catherine joined the Mantellate, a lay branch of the Dominican order dedicated to service. Like the beguines, the Mantellate was a third order that did not take permanent vows but sought a life of personal piety and active service in the world. One scholar has observed that this order gave Catherine a "border zone identity" that enabled her to live a semireligious life with a relative amount of freedom to contemplate and be engaged in the world.[3] Unlike the beguines Mechthild and Hadewijch, Catherine did not live with her religious community, but remained at home and from there sought to build a life and ministry in line with her religious calling.

From the very start, her life was filled with struggle. Catherine was born a twin, but her sister died while Catherine managed to survive. As a child she had an experience of religious calling and vowed herself to virginity. Her family, having lost all their other daughters, wanted her to marry. For years she battled with them, trying every way she could to discourage their efforts, including cutting off her hair, enduring life-threatening fasts, and scalding herself. In return her parents made her a servant in their home, but Catherine did not give up her calling. After an illness left her disfigured, her family relented to her desire and Catherine was allowed to enter the order of the Mantellate.

Catherine spent the next three years in solitude and silence in her own room. The fasting that she had endured to win her freedom had now become a way of life, and she seemed destined to live a life of prayer and ascetic practice. Then at the age of twenty-one she had an experience of mystical marriage to Christ, who ordered her to come out of her room and rejoin her family at the dinner table. From there she began a period of ministry in her surrounding neighborhood by nursing the sick, feeding the hungry, and gaining a reputation for holiness that attracted a crowd of followers. Meanwhile, the struggles around her increased. Her father died and the family business failed. A famine took siege over Siena. In the midst of all this strife, Catherine's visionary experiences deepened until she had a deathlike experience during which she heard Mary assure her that if she agreed to come back to life God would free souls because of her pain (*L*, 2.6.214).[4]

At this point Catherine turned to a life of willing suffering for the world. Her first trip was to Florence, where the Dominican order confirmed the authenticity of her unusual calling and appointed Raymond of Capua to become her confessor. She returned to Siena to tend the sick during another outbreak of the plague and then traveled to Pisa and finally Avignon to encourage the pope to return to Rome. In 1377, when she was thirty, the Avignon papacy ended and Catherine focused her efforts on founding a monastery to house her growing number of followers. Before long, the pope died and she was once again flung into the middle of international events. In Florence she was almost murdered in a papal uprising, but she survived and was called to Rome by the new pope to help garner support for his cause. The last months of her life were spent in Rome amidst crumbling support for the papacy. In January of 1380 she began a month-long hunger strike in an effort to atone for the sins of the church, while the pope was physically attacked by local critics and Italy was at war over papal control. By the end of February she was paralyzed, and on 29 April she died at the age of thirty-three.

Despite the brevity of her life, Catherine had unusual power and influence, especially for a medieval woman. That she was aware of the unusual nature of her life is evident in the account of her call to public ministry. She complained to God about the restrictions placed on women in her day, noting that "propriety forbids a woman to mix so freely in the company of men." In return God told her that "there is no longer male and female, nor lower class and upper class; for all stand equal in my sight, and all things are equally in my power" (*L*, 2.1.121–122). As a result she was instructed to take on an abnormal way of life, totally different from the common run of men or women. She would be freed from the conventional restraints of women and would be able to "mingle freely" with men and women in the mission of saving souls (*L*, 2.5.165).

These assurances from God empowered Catherine to action, but did not keep her from receiving the very criticism she had feared. The sisters in her order did not like the fact that she mingled freely in the world. They told her that traveling was unbecoming for a maiden of the religious life. "Why is that one gadding about so much?" they wondered. "She's a woman. Why doesn't she stay in her cell, if it's God she wants to serve?" (*L*, 3.4.365; also see 3.1.333). From the beginning of her religious life, when she defied convention by remaining in solitude for three years, to her public ministry, which stretched the limits of public service, Catherine broke all expectations of the proper religious life.

Like Margery's, Catherine's piety also stretched the limits of acceptable religious expression. Catherine was considered a nuisance by others, and she endured harassment because of her ecstatic trances. She was charged with trying to be more pious than Jesus and faking her visions (see *L*, 2.5.172). Her fasting was one area that received a lot of criticism. In one letter she admitted that she knew her critics had a point but that there was nothing she could do about her inability to eat except pray to God to help her overcome her weakness (*LN*, 79). As her biographer notes, her critics were "obstinately set on making her keep to the beaten path that suits the common run of men" (*L*, 1.9.80).

The criticism of her public life and pious practice might have ended her religious career had Raymond of Capua not been appointed as her confessor.

A noted Dominican leader and trained theologian, Raymond was able to give Catherine the status she needed to keep her critics at bay as well as a dialogue partner to deepen her teaching and faith. Their friendship lasted for six years, and it was Raymond who wrote her biography and began the movement for her sainthood. He noted that even he doubted her authority until he had a vision of her talking to him as a bearded man who symbolized Christ (see *L*, 1.9.90–91). Thus convinced of her authority, Raymond gave Catherine his undying support, and Catherine was able to lay aside all restraints to save souls.

Catherine's writing was an extension of her public ministry. Her main work is a treatise entitled *The Dialogue*, which records a conversation between God and the soul about the nature of the spiritual life. Dictating this document at the time she was establishing her monastery, Catherine sought to encourage and instruct those under her direction. The text is written with God as the narrator and contains the central elements of Catherine's understanding of suffering. The practice of this teaching can be seen in her two other works, her prayers and letters. The prayers, twenty-six in all, were written down as she prayed aloud. Dictated during the last years of her life, they reveal Catherine's increasing struggle with the evils of her day and her effort to suffer for others. The nearly 400 letters were written in the last six years of her life. Addressed to a wide range of people, they provide a sense of the range of Catherine's influence and a broader sense of her authority and mission. After her death, her followers collected and distributed her letters as instructions in faith, editing out many of the details pertaining to the original recipient.

The Life of Catherine was written between 1385 and 1395 by Raymond as an effort to record the remarkable events of Catherine's life, with the hope that the church would see the saintly nature of her life and work. While containing many historical details, its main purpose was to continue the work of reform and renewal of the church that Catherine had begun in her life. It gives us valuable insight into how Catherine's life of suffering was understood in her own day and age as a life of meaning and virtue.

Through Raymond's efforts Catherine's fame grew. Even before her death she was the most famous holy woman in Italy. *The Dialogue* and *The Life* became popular works after her death. When translated into English, *The Dialogue* was depicted as instruction for the life of enclosure and contemplation while Catherine's active political role was ignored. When she was declared a saint and later patroness of Rome and Italy, the focus was on her work to bring the pope back to Rome, not the power of her spirituality. When Paul VI declared her a doctor of the Church in 1970, he cited her emphasis on Jesus crucified and her obedience to the church, not her unprecedented female authority. As her fame grew, the fullness of Catherine's life with its power and its suffering fell into obscurity. Ironically, the most famous of medieval women is the hardest to recover from the legends of history.

Raymond himself understood the difficulty of the task and states at the beginning of his work that to understand Catherine we must understand the outer and the inner nature of her life. "One would almost say there were two Catherines there: the outer one, in the body, worn to a thread by suffering; and the inner one, in the spirit, strong to keep that body on its feet, and filling it with energy" (*L*, 1.6.66). If we are to recover Catherine's life from the obscurity of history and struggle with the meaning of her life as a model of satisfaction, we must follow Raymond's advice. Catherine is a paradox of outer suffering and inner strength.

THE OUTER SUFFERING OF THE SATISFIED LIFE

The greatest challenge that Catherine presents to us is her willingness to take on suffering to pay for sin. Raymond notes that the purpose of the Mantellate was making satisfaction for their sins by the practice of penance (*L*, 1.8.78). He frames the story of Catherine's early life as the perfection of this calling. She exposed herself to the scalding waters of the sulfur baths (in the hopes of making herself undesirable for marriage) believing that she could exchange the pain she deserved in purgatory for the physical pain she willingly endured on earth (*L*, 1.7.70). Even as an adult she willingly underwent torturous practices of bingeing and purging food as a means of penance. When Raymond urged her to stop eating altogether to save herself from pain, she replied that she saw this as an opportunity "to satisfy her Creator by paying (God) a finite debt" for her sins (*L*, 2.5.177). Later, she imagined that Christ asked her to choose between a crown of thorns and a crown of gold, saying that she could wear one now and would wear the other after death. She grabbed the crown of thorns, declaring that in this life she would take suffering to herself for the refreshment of her soul (*L*, 2.4.158). In these and many other examples Catherine seems to accept and even seek out suffering to satisfy God.

As her public ministry increased, Catherine began to take on suffering to pay for other people's sins as well as her own. When the warring factions of the church spiraled out of control, she saw her role as not only mediating peace, but paying for the consequences of their sins. Catherine urged a church official to ask for mercy for his sins, declaring that she knew God for-gave him because she had assumed the debts of his sins herself (*LN*, 157). While she counseled political leaders, military leaders, church leaders, and anyone else whose sins she saw as threatening the stability of the church, her greatest concern was for the welfare of the pope, and her greatest suffering was on his behalf. "Let my bones be split apart for those for whom I am pray-ing, if such is your will," she prayed. "Let my bones and marrow be ground up for your vicar on earth" (*P*, 1). When all of her efforts seemed in vain, her petitions increased, asking God to use her body as an anvil on which the sins of the pope's adversaries could be hammered out (*P*, 25). That day she began a thirty-day fast that would end her life.

In *The Dialogue* Catherine sets the meaning of suffering within the con-text of the sinfulness of humanity and the justice of God. Infected by the sin of Adam's disobedience, which Catherine describes as "stinking pus" that has infected the whole human race, humanity declared war on God's mercy and became the enemy of God (*D*, 22; 13). While Catherine describes sin at var-ious times as pride, selfish love, disordered will, nonbeing, and sensuality, it is at base a perversion of our humanness and a denial of our relationship with God.[5] It is a poison that pollutes our nature and poisons the world (*D*, 17). Just as the plague had overcome Europe, so sin had overtaken human life.

Having seen the devastation of war, Catherine knew that the war between humanity and God could not be reconciled without the restoration of justice. So Christ came to earth as mediator, taking on himself the pun-ishment for humanity's injustice. While she does not clearly articulate why, Catherine states that divine justice demands suffering in atonement for sin, and by suffering in the body on the cross Christ placates God's anger (*D*, 13–14). Thus she prays, "You turned our great war with God into a great peace" (*P*, 1). It is this belief in the centrality of God's justice that undergirds Catherine's own acts of suffering. Justice demands payment for sin, and the ongoing sins of humanity demand the continued suffering of sinners. It is faith in the uncompromising justice of God that compels her to suffer for oth-ers. In her last prayer, just weeks before her death, Catherine prays, "My Lord, since it is impossible that your justice should be set aside . . . whatever pun-ishment is due to this people, let it be worked out upon this body of mine" (*L*, 3.2.346).

Catherine believes she can suffer for others because Christ serves not only as the mediator but the model for our salvation. She describes Christ as a bridge to salvation, reconciling the world to God and providing a straight path for our own life of faith. "I made of him a bridge for you," God declares, "because the road to heaven had been destroyed. If you travel along this delightful straight way, which is a lightsome truth, holding the key of obedience, you will pass through the world's darknesses without stumbling. And in the end you will unlock heaven with the Word's key" (D, 166). Christ's body is stretched out from earth to heaven, giving Christians a way through the perils of life. Outside his path is the way of disobedience that poisons the soul. The key to heaven is walking along the way of Christ's obedience even unto death.

Obedience is the theme of the last section of *The Dialogue* and the main theme of Raymond's record of Catherine's life. It is obedience that satisfies God's justice and reconciles humanity to God. Obedience to God modeled on the bridge of Christ compels Catherine to defy her family, work tirelessly for the good of others, and suffer for the sins of the world. One of the best-known examples of Catherine's obedience is her caring for a sick woman named Andrea. Sickened by her cancerous sore, Catherine forced herself to suck from the wound to overcome her revulsion (L, 2.4.155). Whether true story or legend, the account serves as an example of the lengths to which Catherine was willing to go to live out the obedience of Christ. It also parallels the three stages of obedience, which Catherine describes as the three steps of the bridge of Christ. At his feet one is stripped of the sin of disobedience, at the heart of Christ one is dressed in love, and at the mouth of Christ one finds the peace of perfect obedience (D, 26). In service to Andrea, Catherine tastes the mouth of her bridge.

The symbol of this obedience is the blood of Christ, which becomes a central metaphor for Catherine of the sacrificial love of obedience. As one commentator notes, "At whatever point we enter her mind we encounter Christ crucified, and in particular the thought of his blood."[6] It is the blood of Christ that nourishes her soul as the model of suffering and as the food of communion. While many medieval mystics focus on the passion of Christ, Catherine takes this imagery to new heights. In one of her most graphic visions Christ rewards her suffering on behalf of the sick by allowing her to drink from his side. "Drawn close in this way to the outlet of the Fountain of Life, she fastened her lips upon that sacred wound, and still more eagerly the mouth of her soul, and there she slaked her mystic thirst for long and long" (L, 2.4.163). Thus strengthened by the blood of Christ, Catherine was encouraged to continue her work.

This emphasis on blood was Catherine's way of responding to the bloody suffering of her day. Having worked in the plague, Catherine was surrounded by the blood of the sick. Witnessing the warfare of the church, Catherine had seen the blood of its victims. In a letter to Raymond, Catherine recounts her presence at the execution of a young man caught in the civil wars of Siena. She held his head in her lap as he was decapitated. Then she writes to Raymond that she saw Jesus open his side and receive the blood of the man into his own blood, thus sanctifying his blood in Christ. She remained on the platform bathed in the fragrance of blood. When she opens this and many of her letters with greetings "in the precious blood of God's Son" she means that she is aware of the reality of blood (*LN*, 108–11).

Catherine is indeed worn to a thread by her suffering, and she takes much of it on in obedience to the justice of God and the example of Christ in order to eradicate sin. It is a suffering that appears to be based on a theology of satisfying a wrathful and bloodthirsty God. Raymond presents her life as a perfection of Christian faith, which reinforces the idea that self-sacrifice is the means toward reconciliation with God. It is obvious that her later designation as a saint and doctor of the Church is due to the fact that her actions reinforced the dominant ideology of satisfactionary atonement. But did she herself find strength in this understanding of satisfaction, or did she understand the satisfaction of suffering within a framework of God's satisfying love? Answering this question will allow us to see how Catherine challenges rather than merely contradicts a feminist theology of atonement. For this question we must turn to a study of the inner strength of Catherine of Siena.

THE INNER STRENGTH OF THE SATISFIED LIFE

While a review of the life of Catherine suggests that suffering is the way to satisfaction, a study of *The Dialogue* reveals that it is not suffering that is the key, but the inner desire for God that lies behind it. Thus she notes that suffering makes one sad and happy. One is sad at the physical pain caused by suffering but happy at the desire for charity that underlies the work. Thus she calls suffering "fattening sadness" because it can increase the inner spirit and make love grow (*D*, 78). It is not suffering but the desire behind it that has value. Behind suffering is love for God born of the knowledge of God's goodness and the desire to eradicate the sin in oneself and others that denies that goodness (*D*, 4). Thus, Catherine is able to make the startling claim that she longs for suffering, not because she desires pain, but because she desires God. Suffering is endured for the glory and praise of God (*D*, 78).

Catherine's willingness to suffer is based on the pragmatic realization that in this life one cannot avoid pain. No one passes through life without suffering, she writes. The difference is that the servants of God suffer physically but not in their spirit, while the wicked suffer physically and spiritually. The difference is a matter of one's will being in conflict with God or in union with God. For the latter, suffering rests in the confidence that the soul is at one with the will of God. Since her suffering is understood within the framework of desiring God, she concludes that suffering does not make her weary because her will is "in tune" with God's will (*D*, 45). The servants of God feel no grief in suffering but rather feel God in the soul and are satisfied (*D*, 48). God promises her that "in any situation or at any time whatever . . . I know how to and can and will satisfy her in wonderful ways" (*D*, 142). Filled with this reassurance, Catherine's spirit cannot suffer and she remains strong.

In her advice to others Catherine is careful not to lift up her suffering but rather her desire for God as exemplary. In a letter to one of her followers she writes that perfection does not consist in mortifying and killing one's body, but in killing perverse self-will. The goal is not to seek suffering but to devote one's infinite desire to the honor of God and the salvation of souls. We nourish ourselves, Catherine concludes, at the table of holy desire (*LP*, 265–66). In another letter Catherine is more explicit, advising against fasting if the body is weak. Whether she wants others to avoid the dangers of fasting that have befallen her, or merely wants to remind others that her own life is not a model for others, is not clear. What is clear is that she wants to emphasize the proper understanding of her follower's desire. "Discretion," she writes "proposes that penance be done as a means and not as a principal desire" (*LP*, 268). The principal desire is to enact God's will.

While desire for God makes suffering satisfying, it is Catherine's knowledge of herself as created in the image of a loving God that makes desire possible. "In the gentle mirror of God she sees her own dignity: that through no merit of hers but by his creation she is the image of God" (*D*, 13). This "cell of self-knowledge," as Catherine calls it, serves as the foundation of her strength. It is her sense of dignity that carries her through her struggle with her family, that gives her the confidence to follow a unique form of religious calling, and that empowers her to counsel popes and kings. Like many medieval mystics she describes the image of God as the image of the Trinity in her soul. It is the ability to remember, understand, and will the goodness of God that is the mirror of God. As one turns inside oneself to the truth of one's being, there one finds God. "You gave us our will so that we might be able to love what our understanding has seen and what our memory has held" (P, 20). The truth of self-knowledge allows Catherine to see the God in her as her true nature and all that counters this will as sin. Thus, she notes, we have to strip ourselves of will to take on the gentle will of God as one "turns one's garment inside out when one undresses" (P, 11). Inside the rebelliousness of will that is the poison of sin is the goodness of will to love God.

The foundation of this will is the memory of God's love. While both Raymond and Catherine talk about appeasing God's justice, the deeper reality for Catherine is that God is not a wrathful judge but a Gentle First Truth, a truth of love. Catherine realizes that her desire for God comes from God's desire for her. In fact, she suggests that God is mad with love for creation. In *The Dialogue* she writes, "O mad lover! And you have need of your creature? It seems so to me, for you act as if you could not live without her. . . . You are pleased and delighted over her within yourself, as if you were drunk with desire for her salvation" (D, 153). As Linda Woolsey notes, the powerful God that Catherine imagines as just becomes vulnerable through love.[7] It is this vulnerability that gives Catherine confidence in God even in suffering. God tells her, "Daughter think of me; if you do, instantly I will think of you." She remains confident that if she remembers God's love, she will remember that she rests in God's watchful care (L, 1.10. 98).

The nature of this divine care becomes clear in understanding the passion of Christ. Christ is more than the mediator of salvation; he stands as the vehicle of the love that accomplishes our salvation. Christ tends the wound of sin like a wet nurse who drinks the bitter medicine of the passion in order to pass on to humanity the wholeness of life. Like medicine that is too strong to be digested except through the nurse's milk, the cure for the disease of sin must come to us through the body of Christ (D, 14). It is a painful cure, but one that heals the human race from the disease of sin. Only the scar and weakness from sin remain, which can be healed in baptism and strengthened in the ongoing nourishment of the church.

Thus the love of God comes to us in the nourishment of the body of Christ in communion. Christ is the food of souls, strengthening the image of

God in the soul and teaching the soul to understand the nature of God's love. God is the table that lays out the food; the Holy Spirit is the waiter that serves the food (*D*, 78). In the understanding of the passion as the vehicle of salvation and nourishment of divine love, Catherine is strengthened and energized. Her letters end with the refrain, "Gentle Jesus! Jesus love!" and in this greeting is the realization that in Jesus one understands the first truth of divine love.

It is the memory of the goodness of God as our essential humanity and the understanding that we are healed in the passion of Christ that gives Catherine the will to love. As she notes in one of her letters, those who eat at the table of God become like the food they eat, working for God's honor and the salvation of others (*LN*, 50). The response to salvation is not just perfect obedience but perfect love. This fourth stage of faith is a perfect union with God in which the love of God is engrafted onto the heart of humanity. Catherine describes this union as like a fish in the sea in which water and fish intermingle (*P*, 2). Or at other times she talks about the elements in a loaf of bread kneaded together until the individual ingredients are indistinguishable and a new reality emerges (*P*, 14). More often Catherine speaks of Christ as engrafted onto the dead tree of humanity, thus enabling humanity to bear new fruit (*P*, 17).

For Catherine, this union was so complete that she imagined herself engrafted with the heart of Christ. In response to her petition to have a clean heart created within, she imagined her side opened and her heart carried away by God. A few days later she experienced another vision in which she saw her side opened again and the heart of Christ placed inside (*L*, 2.6.179–180). At another point she saw her heart entering Christ's side and becoming one with his heart (*L*, 2.6.186). This mingling of hearts led her to greater and greater acts of love for others, confident in the will to love in Christ. Filled with the heart of Christ, she walked into all situations confident of the will of God.

One of the effects of this union of hearts was a powerful ability to demand mercy from God. Raymond records numerous accounts in which Catherine was able to pray for healing. During the plague he himself was revived by her prayer on his behalf (*L*, 2.8.255). At her sister's death, Catherine's prayers released her from purgatory (*L*, 1.4.45). At her father's death her petition was more pronounced, and Catherine would not relent until God allowed her to take on her father's sins so that he could be released from purgatory. Raymond notes that Catherine wrestled with God, who held out for the demands of justice while she pleaded for the work of grace (*L*, 2.7.221). At her mother's impending death Catherine's prayer was bolder still. "Lord this is not what you promised me," she declared, and her mother was revived to life (*L*, 2.8.244). Truly God is vulnerable in love, and Catherine is able to tap into the resources of that love, despite the demands of justice. "Nature bowed to God's command," Raymond notes, "issued through the mouth of Catherine" (*L*, 2.8.247). And in the end the ways of love always triumphed.

But that does not mean that Catherine could save the world. As the state of the church declined in the months following the schism over papal leadership, Catherine became increasingly aware of the limits of her ability to love. When ordered to Rome by the pope she came and delivered a stirring speech to the bishops that impressed even the pope with her courageous spirit (*L*, 3.1.334). But when her health failed and there was nothing else to do, she prayed for her heart to be crushed and its blood squeezed out upon the church. Yet even in this desperate act Catherine remained confident of the saving work of God. Evil will be defeated, she writes, "not by what our bodies suffer, but by virtue of the glowing measureless Charity of God" (*LK*, 276–77). With these hopeful words, she ended her last letter to Raymond.

With this image of the bleeding heart we return to the centrality of the idea of blood. More than a symbol of sacrifice, blood is a symbol of the deep connection between humanity and divinity, oneself and one's neighbors. Blood is the sign of love. It is Christ's blood that waters the tree of humanity so that we might bear fruit (*P*, 17). We are baptized into his blood and receive the nourishment of his blood in communion. It is blood that is above all the sign of the union of humanity and divinity, which "calls every believer to enter into the mystery not only as redeemed but as co-redeemer."[8] It is the flow of blood that empowers the soul to act in love for God.

Blood also represents the healing power of love in life. Given the context of her day, in which bloodletting was the primary form of medical treatment, it is not surprising that blood was associated with healing for Catherine. Just as the letting of blood was believed to draw off "corrupt matter from the body,"[9] so the blood of Christ is able to draw off the corruption of sin. It is "in his blood" that Catherine acts in the world to mediate family rivalries, reconcile civil discord, and work for the healing of the corruption of the church. As Elizabeth Petroff notes, "the healing power of blood was constantly revealed to her in ordinary brutal life."[10] Blood is a symbol of hope that no matter how broken the world, the blood of God works to nourish life.

Beneath the outer suffering of Catherine there is a spirit of connectedness that unites her to the world and to God in the confidence of the love of God manifest in the midst of the pain of life. It is a love that she can depend on, be united with, and desire for the good of the world. Certainly it is an inner spirit that endures much for the sake of love, but it is in desire and hope that her spirit rests. Therefore, she can write that seeing God, she loves; "loving, she is satisfied; being satisfied, she knows the truth; knowing the truth, her will is grounded firmly in (God)—so firmly and solidly that nothing can cause her to suffer, for she is in possession of what she had longed for, to see (God) and to see (God's) name praised and glorified" (*D*, 82). In possession of such satisfying truth she is energized.

CONTEMPORARY REFLECTIONS

How are we to put together this picture of the outer suffering and inner strength of Catherine? The uncommon nature of her life has perplexed interpreters and continues to elude most scholars today. The vast amount of literature on Catherine tends to polarize around a condemnation of her outer asceticism or a veneration of her inner spirit. At the worst she is merely a medieval victim of anorexia that leads us to condemn not only her practice, but the entire base of religious belief that undergirds her faith. At the other extreme she is a free, loving, joyous figure of self-determination who is a precursor of the feminist spirit. In the middle are a few scholars who try to see the active nature of her suffering in the context of a spiritual vision that is fully engaged in the world.[11]

In light of this study into the meaning of suffering as a model of the satisfied life, the question is how Catherine's life of outer suffering and inner satisfaction might broaden our understanding of the satisfied life and even challenge our understanding of the satisfying love of God. Is there any truth to Bynum's thesis that medieval mystics like Catherine challenge us with the possibility that suffering is fruitful?

Certainly suffering was a common experience of all the mystics in this study. Margery suffered much in her search for satisfaction and found comfort in the idea that in suffering she could identify with Christ. Likewise, Hadewijch's life of service led her to a suffering exile in which the idea of carrying the cross gave her the hope to endure her persecution. However, neither understood suffering as a means to satisfaction, but rather as a consequence of their searching and serving lives. The role of suffering in their lives is nothing like it is in Catherine's life. While they endure suffering, Catherine seeks suffering. Her hope is not that in suffering Christ is present, but that in her suffering is the presence of Christ. It is the experience of suffering itself that satisfies her. As she suffers, she models the obedience of Christ that atones for sin. In suffering she steps onto the bridge of Christ.

It is the idea that outer suffering atones for sin that most challenges our study. We began with the problem of believing that self-sacrificial love could earn satisfaction. Roberta Bondi suggests the problem of atonement is in the mistaken idea that we are unworthy and need to earn love from God or from others. Julian argued that Christ suffers to satisfy us of God's enduring love, but we do not suffer in return. There is no need, since there is nothing to appease in God's sight. Anger is merely a human projection of unworthiness onto God. Thus Julian argues that we are not to dwell on suffering, but to trust that all happens within the embrace of God's love. Living during the same time frame as Catherine, Julian sought to deemphasize the idea that the plague was a divine judgment for sin.

Catherine's theology, as it has been handed down to us by her recorders, does emphasize the idea that suffering can placate God's anger. Justice requires payment for sin, and the crucifixion of Christ, along with the ongoing suffering of human beings, is part of the justice of God. But in her prayers on behalf of those who suffer she presents a different understanding of God as vulnerable in mercy. Remember that her prayers wrestle with the reality of justice and mercy. While God calls for justice, she calls for mercy and argues until the mercy of God relents. Only then does she take on the suffering of others. The picture of Catherine that emerges is one that is filled with self-determination, not unworthiness.

Key to understanding the suffering of Catherine is the cell of self-knowledge that underlies her suffering. It is the knowledge that we are created in the image of God with the memory of God's goodness, the understanding of the passion as the lengths to which love will go, and the will to realize fully the depths of our desire to live in unity with that love that motivates Catherine's life. Underlying her actions is not the master-slave relationship that is the basis of the satisfactionary model of atonement but a relationship of identity with the love of God. This basic insight returns to Julian's marveling at the courtesy of God that transforms the divine-human relationship.

Catherine calls it the mad love of God. It is this inner identity of her self in God that propels Catherine to the outer suffering that made her famous.

Which leads us back to some interesting insights about suffering as a possible mode of the satisfied life. First and foremost we must not glorify her self-inflicted suffering. Catherine herself prayed to God to overcome her weakness and advised her admirers not to follow her example. Given the epidemic of eating disorders in our day, the outer suffering of Catherine's life must be recognized and mourned. Once I made the mistake of naively including the discussion of Catherine in an undergraduate course of Christian leaders and was shocked when a young woman confessed to me her problem with anorexia and asked me why we were studying a Christian who had the same problem. I had to admit that Mary Solberg is right when she observes that the value of suffering is not liberating to victims of violence. It merely protects God and those who benefit from the suffering of others. Catherine was mistaken when she said that she sought to satisfy her Creator in her bingeing and purging, and we should do all we can to eradicate the theological justification that leads to such action.

It is not surprising that given the theological climate of her day and the lack of opportunity for study, Catherine would adopt the dominant theology of satisfying the justice of God. What is surprising is that she would dare to argue with this theology, even to argue with God. She wrestled with the idea of God's justice and demanded that God act with mercy. She was confident that God's love seeks us out and desires our salvation. She was sure that her own will working in concert with God could free souls. This confidence led her to suffer on behalf of others as a work of protest against the sin of the world. It raises for us the possibility that suffering is satisfying because it connects us with the work of God in the world.

Catherine stands as a reminder that the satisfied life is not an easy life of feeling good, not a life of indifference or escape, but rather a life that realizes salvation in the midst of brokenness. It is a life of full engagement with the world. In her book on suffering, Dorothee Soelle writes that the acceptance of suffering is a "part of the great yes to life." It is understanding the nature of the reality that we carry out the act of suffering or we are passive recipients of suffering, indifferent as stones.[12] Catherine realized that suffering is not an option in life. What is an option is whether we will have the courage to be fully engaged in the suffering of our day in solidarity with others and with God. She refused to be indifferent to plague victims, casualties of the civil war of Siena, the corruption of the church, or the political infighting of her day. From her unwavering care of Andrea to her support of a criminal at the guillotine, Catherine showed suffering as a life wholly engaged in the world.

Catherine also challenges us to realize fully the depths of what it means to understand oneself as wholly connected to God and to the world. Hildegard spoke of the realm of justice as the greening of God that slowly seeps into our souls and throughout the world as a flow of love and virtue. For Catherine the image is one of the flow of blood, which connects us to God and to one another. The blood of Christ is a reminder for her of the saving work of God at work in the suffering of the world. It is a suffering that results from the depth of God's connection to creation, of God's vulnerability of love. Likewise she suffers for others because she realizes that the sins of one affect the whole. Here Catherine gives us the possibility of rethinking the meaning of the blood of Christ, especially in communion, as an image of connectedness. Like the power that flows in and through the world, the blood of Christ reminds us of the power of God in and through the pain of life. The crucifixion is the power of connectedness at work in the world. For Catherine the blood of Christ provides a power in suffering, a power of the image of God in her life working for the reconciliation of the world.

One of Catherine's most fruitful ideas is the nature of Christ's saving work. While the idea of Christ as our bridge and therefore our role model is more prevalent in her writing, the theme of Christ as wet nurse is more thought-provoking. As wet nurse Christ provides the medicine for our salvation in a manner that puts his own body in service for humanity. The flow of blood, like the flow of milk, contains the life-giving elements of wholeness. The wet nurse mediates salvation in a bodily form. Like Hildegard, Catherine sees the work of Christ leading toward a healing of the world. In communion that healing continues and gives us the food to be reconciled and reconcilers for God in the world.

So in the end we have to consider the possibility that suffering can be fruitful. Both Catherine and Julian lived in the midst of great suffering, and both had to find a way to live within their world. Julian figured out the inner meaning that God does not cause us to suffer for our salvation. Catherine lived the reality that once we realize our identity with God, our inner strength can propel us to live fully in our times. To consider suffering for others as satisfaction is the limit of the love of God. It may also be the limit of satisfaction. It makes us realize that the saints of all days—the Catherines, the Mother Teresas, the Oscar Romeros, the common people suffering in base Christian communities, in urban ghettos, in health care clinics, and with the rural poor—challenge feminists to ponder anew the claim that we are satisfied in God's love. The fruit of salvation is the healing not only of us but of our world.

chapter eight

BEING AT HOME WITH
OURSELVES IN GOD

In her recent book, *Women and Redemption*, Rosemary Radford Ruether summarizes the entire history of the theology of redemption to show how feminist theology challenges the doctrine of atonement. She concludes that feminist theologians agree that there is no need for the idea of an outside mediator who saves us from our sinful condition. Rather, men and women are created equally in the image of God. Sin is found in external structures of domination that deny this truth, and redemption is the work of transforming these structures. Thus we are called to the work of saving ourselves.[1] Figures from the past such as Julian, Mechthild, Hildegard, Margery, Hadewijch, and Catherine can show feminist theology where we have come from, but they do not serve as sources for contemporary reflection because they still hold on to an idea of salvation as divine work.

But there is more to sin than Ruether admits, and thus we need a vision of the divine work of salvation. We are indeed created in the image of God, but we need to be saved from the dissatisfaction that this image is tarnished and the conclusion that we are not worthy of God's love. Ruether's answer is to denounce the reality of sin as the cause of this dissatisfaction. My suggestion is to name the reality of denying the goodness of our creation as sin. Sin is blindness to God's love, which leads to self-blame and the projection of self-wrath onto God. Julian calls it the sharpest scourge of self-hate. Sometimes sin is manifested as the refusal of love, interrupting the flow of

God's love. Here Mechthild talks about pride and anger as manifestations of trying to control love. While control is a more active form of sin, it is still caused by blindness to the nature of love. The widest manifestation of this blindness is acting without regard for the circle of God's love in creation. Whether sin is understood as acts of omission or acts of self-absorption, Hildegard describes sin as this blindness to the larger reality in which we live. Sin is not just an external problem of domination; it is the internalization and subsequent manifestation of this domination in us, in our relation with God, in our work in the world.

If sin is the dissatisfaction of God's love, then we need to be satisfied that God loves us. It is the work of God that must break into our limited vision and satisfy us of our worthiness in the eyes of God. Realizing that satisfaction is a human need, and that it is divine work, is the central insight for a feminist theology of atonement. Christ asks Julian if she is satisfied, Hadewijch advises her beguines that only God's love can satisfy us, and Hildegard claims that we find satisfaction in the taste of God in communion and the touch of God in acts of virtue. Satisfaction is primarily the work of divine love. This redefinition critiques Anselm's understanding of atonement as paying back honor to God. To be satisfied is to realize that salvation is accomplished by divine initiative, not human effort. The mad love of God seeks us out, longs for courteous relation with us, and works in and through our lives to empower us with the eschatological vision of our redemption.

This work is accomplished in Christ, who reveals the unconditional nature of God's love and works to cultivate this relationship of love in our hearts. Julian reminds us that the crucifixion is part, but not all, of this cultivating work. Mechthild shows us how the crucifixion and resurrection stand together as an image of suffering transformed. The suffering of Christ is witness to the power of God working in and through rather than over the world. It is a power that persuades but does not control us, a power that cannot be thwarted by suffering. For Julian, Christ stands as the vehicle of satisfying love that works like a gardener to cultivate our salvation.

This work of Christ lives on in the church, especially in the act of communion, which Julian calls the milk of salvation and Hildegard proclaims is satisfying drink. Like a sponge, Christ absorbs death into his body and heals us from sin. Catherine likens Christ to a wet nurse who passes on to us the medicine of salvation in her milk. In communion we are nourished with the food of salvation. Julian reminds us that we need the community of faith to witness to the saving love of God and to help enlarge our individual limited vision of reality.

It is this vision of the larger world that is the goal of salvation. It begins in the world of courteous relation with God. As we realize the potential of being the friend of God, trusting and feeding on our friendship, we learn to see ourselves through the gaze of God. Such a vision allows us to break free of the limitations of the world's vision of our lives. As Mechthild rests in the forsakenness of God, she learns to act in courageous ways that defy societal limitations. Likewise, she learns that the love of God is not a domineering or dominated love. Such courteous relation serves as a training ground for the larger circle of God's love in creation. The just order of our relationship with God serves as a model for the just relations of the world. Therefore, Hildegard calls us gardens in bloom. The joy of such a life of virtue is the highest form of satisfaction.

One intriguing aspect of this study is the suggestion that Mary is the model of satisfaction. Mechthild sees the crucial role of Mary as lover and wife of God, while Hadewijch describes the humility of Mary as the power to tame God. Margery identifies with the motherly nature of Mary to mourn with and for her son, Jesus. Taken together these images of Mary's love, humility, and compassion enlarge our understanding of the possibilities of satisfaction. The satisfied life is neither a passive life nor a life that is merely a vessel of divine love. Satisfaction is not the "fulfillment" Mary Daly describes as a plastic passion and perversion of the meaning of true joy.[2] It is an embodiment of the possibility of union with the powerful love of God

To be satisfied is the most rewarding and hardest work. For Margery it was work that sent her to new places and new identities in the search for her worth in the sight of God. Her story is the story of many Christian women who search for a way to find satisfaction in the midst of the many relationships of their lives. My hope is that this book will serve as encouragement in the same way that Julian encouraged Margery to trust in her journey, seek her own identity, and stay in communion with the church. Surrounded by the witness of Christian women such as Margery, we can take comfort in the knowledge that the satisfying love of God is within reach. The reward of such a life is a growing satisfaction in being at home with ourselves in God.

Such a life can take us to new heights of leadership as Christians. For Hadewijch that leadership took the form of service. Liberated from the guilt of Christian drudgery, service can be a noble deed. The fighting spirit of

Hadewijch can inspire us all to break free of the stereotypes of feminine service and reclaim this image with pride as an active embodiment of the satisfying love of God. Desire for the good can be a manifestation of the satisfying life. In such desire is the energy to venture into new forms of leadership in full-grown love. Hadewijch is an inspiration for the ever increasing numbers of women who seek leadership and service in the church. She is also a model of androgyny that is worth consideration for women and men. She reminds us that the satisfied life can find joy in service and with it the love of God.

A satisfied life also challenges us to full engagement in the world. Few of us will reach the heights of engagement that characterized Catherine's life, and few of us will be called to the depths of suffering that she willingly endured on behalf of love. It is Catherine who stands most outside our world, which is obsessed with self-development. And yet she is the one who found her strength in the cell of self-knowledge. Knowing that we are created in the image of the Trinity as relational creatures living in relation with the relation of Creativity reminds us that the satisfaction of our lives is bound up with the satisfaction of the world. The satisfied life will take us down many roads that counter our individualized, privatized notion of comfort and satisfaction. It will call us to challenge our cultural limitations. It will challenge us to speak up despite the criticism of the church. It will inspire us to follow the mad love of God wherever it will lead.

This life of satisfaction is beyond our experience and vision of the world. It is an eschatological vision that can only come to fruition through the power of God working in our midst. This saving work is woven into the basic story of our faith and illuminated by sages from our past. They stand as a guide for us to see the vastness of the vision of God's love. We who follow in their footsteps can take nourishment in their lives and teaching as we move forward to our own place in the satisfying love of God.

✖ ✖ ✖

※

NOTES

1. ACHIEVING SELF-SATISFACTION?

1. Pamela Dickey Young, "Beyond Moral Influence to an Atoning Life," *Theology Today* 52 (October 1995): 344.

2. Mary Daly, *Beyond God the Father: Toward a Philosophy of Women's Liberation* (Boston: Beacon Press, 1973), 77; Delores Williams, "Black Women's Surrogacy Experience and the Christian Notion of Redemption," in *After Patriarchy: Feminist Transformations of the World Religions*, ed. Paula Cooey, William Eakin, and Jay McDaniel (Maryknoll, N.Y.: Orbis Books, 1991), 9; Mary Solberg, *Compelling Knowledge: A Feminist Proposal for an Epistemology of the Cross* (Albany: State University of New York Press, 1997), 153; Joanne Carlson Brown, "Divine Child Abuse?" *Daughters of Sarah* 18 (summer 1992): 28.

3. Roberta Bondi, *Memories of God: Theological Reflections on a Life* (Nashville: Abingdon, 1995), 134–36, 112–13.

4. Inna Jane Ray, "The Atonement Muddle: An Historical Analysis and Clarification of a Salvation Theory," *Journal of Women and Religion* 15 (1997): 12.

5. See Ted Peters, "Atonement and the Final Scapegoat," *Perspectives in Religious Studies* 19 (summer 1992); Leanne Van Dyk, "Do Theories of Atonement Foster Abuse?" *Dialog* 35 (winter 1996): 24; Delores Williams, "Black Women's Surrogacy Experience and the Christian Notion of Redemption," 11–13; Mary Grey, *Feminism, Redemption, and Christian Tradition* (Mystic, Conn.: Twenty-Third Publications, 1990), 137–51.

6. Paul Fiddes, *Past and Present Salvation: The Christian Idea of Atonement* (Louisville: Westminster/John Knox Press, 1989), 13.

7. See Darby Kathleen Ray, *Deceiving the Devil: Atonement, Abuse, and Ransom* (Cleveland: The Pilgrim Press, 1998).

8. Bernard McGinn, ed., *Meister Eckhart and the Beguine Mystics: Hadewijch of Brabant, Mechthild of Magdeburg, and Marguerite Porete* (New York: Continuum, 1994), 6.

2. JULIAN OF NORWICH ON BEING SATISFIED

1. Joan Nuth, "Two Medieval Soteriologies: Anselm of Canterbury and Julian of Norwich," *Theological Studies* 53 (December 1992): 612. Lillian Bozak-DeLeo notes that this style, which has less logical completeness than traditional theology, is also more in line with the fragmented style of theology in a postmodern world. See "The Soteriology of Julian of Norwich," in *Theology and the University*, ed. John Apczynski (Lanham, Md.: University Press of America, 1987), 38. Others have tried to make a case that Julian employs a feminine style that is more holistic than male theology. See Maria R. Lichtmann, "Julian of Norwich and the Ontology of the Feminine," *Studia Mystica* 13 (March 1990): 53–60.

2. Elizabeth Robertson, "Medieval Medical Views of Women and Female Spirituality in the *Ancrene Wise* and Julian of Norwich's *Showings*," in *Feminist Approaches to the Body in Medieval Literature*, ed. Linda Lomperis and Sarah Stanbury (Philadelphia: University of Pennsylvania Press, 1993), 161.

3. Anselm of Canterbury, *Why God Became Man and the Virgin Conception and Original Sin*, trans. Joseph Colleran (Albany, N.Y.: Magi Books, 1969), 113.

4. Ibid., 84.

5. Ibid.

6. See Timothy Gorringe, *Redeeming Time: Atonement through Education* (London: Darton, Longman, and Todd, 1986), 224–25; Simon Maimela, "The Atonement in the Context of Liberation Theology," *Journal of Theology for Southern Africa* 39 (June 1982): 48.

7. Vincent Brümmer, "Atonement and Reconciliation," *Religious Studies* 28 (December 1992): 446.

8. Lillian Bozak-DeLeo, "The Soteriology of Julian of Norwich," 39.

9. Quotations from Julian's texts are cited in the text with the abbreviations listed below. Each abbreviation is followed by the chapter number from which the quotation is taken.

SHL: *Showings* (Long Text), trans. Edmund Colledge and James Walsh (New York: Paulist Press, 1978).

SHS: *Showings* (Short Text), trans. Edmund Colledge and James Walsh (New York: Paulist Press, 1978).

10. Brant Pelphrey, *Christ Our Mother: Julian of Norwich* (Wilmington, Del.: Michael Glazier, 1989), 33.

11. Brad Peters, "Julian of Norwich and the Internalized Dialogue of Prayer," *Mystics Quarterly* 20 (December 1994): 129.

12. Mary Olson, "God's Inappropriate Grace: Images of Courtesy in Julian of Norwich's *Showings*," *Mystics Quarterly* 20 (June 1994): 58.

13. Andrew Sprung, "'We nevyr shall come out of hyin': Enclosure and Immanence in Julian of Norwich's Book of *Showings*," *Mystics Quarterly* 19 (June 1993): 52.

14. Alexandra Barratt, "How Many Children Had Julian of Norwich? Editions, Translations, and Versions of Her Revelations," in *Vox Mystica: Essays for Valerie M. Lagorio*, ed. Anne Clark Bartlett et al. (Cambridge: D. S. Brewer, 1995), 33.

15. Joan Nuth, "Two Medieval Soteriologies," 640.

16. Ibid., 632.

17. Staley also notes that the gardener image draws on the labor reality in England during Julian's day and would have resonated with the lay audience of her writing. See "Julian of Norwich and the Late Fourteenth-Century Crisis of Authority," in *The Powers of the Holy: Religion, Politics and Gender in Late Medieval English Culture*, ed. David Aers and Lynn Staley (University Park: Pennsylvania State University Press, 1996), 164.

18. David Aers and Lynn Staley, *The Powers of the Holy*, 103–4.

19. Janet Schaller, "Mentoring of Women: Transformation in Adult Religious Education," *Religious Education* 91 (spring 1996): 160–71.

3. MECHTHILD OF MAGDEBURG ON SATISFYING LOVE

1. Elizabeth Petroff, ed., *Medieval Women's Visionary Literature* (New York: Oxford University Press, 1986), 207.

2. Mechthild of Magdeburg, *The Flowing Light of the Godhead*, trans. Frank Tobin, preface by Margot Schmidt (New York: Paulist Press, 1997). Quotations are cited parenthetically in the text and include references to the book number followed by the part number.

3. Oliver Davies, "Transformational Processes in the Work of Julian of Norwich and Mechthild of Magdeburg," in *The Medieval Mystical Tradition in England: Exeter Symposium V*, ed. Marion Glasscoe (Cambridge: D. S. Brewer, 1992), 52.

4. William Seaton, "Transformation of Convention in Mechthild of Magdeburg," *Mystics Quarterly* 10 (June 1984): 67.

5. Amy Hollywood, *The Soul as Virgin Wife: Mechthild of Magdeburg, Marguerite Porete, and Meister Eckhart* (Notre Dame, Ind.: University of Notre Dame Press, 1996), 72–74.

6. Caroline Bynum, *Jesus as Mother: Studies in the Spirituality of the High Middle Ages* (Berkeley: University of California Press, 1982), 233.

7. See Ulrike Wiethaus, "Suffering, Love, and Transformation in Mechthild of Magdeburg," *Listening* 22 (spring 1987): 139–50.

8. Amy Hollywood, *The Soul as Virgin Wife*, 76–84.

9. Johnette Putnam, "Mechthild of Magdeburg: Poet and Mystic," in *Medieval Women Monastics: Wisdom's Wellsprings*, ed. Miriam Schmitt and Linda Kulzer (Collegeville, Minn.: Liturgical Press, 1996), 224.

10. Nadia Lahutsky, "Food and Feminism and Historical Interpretations: The Case of Medieval Holy Women," in *Setting the Table: Women in Theological Conversation*, ed. Rita Nakashima Brock, Claudia Camp, and Serene Jones (St. Louis: Chalice Press, 1995), 235.

11. See Susan Clark, "'Ze Glicher Wis': Mechthild von Magdeburg and the Concept of Likeness," in *The Worlds of Medieval Women: Creativity, Influence, Imagination*, ed. Constance Berman et al. (Morgantown: West Virginia University Press, 1985); Elizabeth Anderson, "Mechthild Von Magdeburg: Her Creativity and Her Audience," in *Women, the Book, and the Godly*, vol. I, ed. Lesley Smith and Jane Taylor (Cambridge: D. S. Brewer, 1995).

12. Emilie Zum Brunn and Georgette Epiney-Burgard, *Women Mystics in Medieval Europe*, trans. Sheila Hughes (New York: Paragon House, 1989), 53.

13. See Sallie McFague, *Models of God: Theology for an Ecological, Nuclear Age* (Philadelphia: Fortress Press, 1987).

14. See Valerie Saiving, "The Human Situation: A Feminine View," *Journal of Religion* 40 (April 1960): 100–12; Roberta Bondi, *Memories of God*, 107–10.

15. Caroline Bynum, *Jesus as Mother*, 178.

16. Ulrike Wiethaus, "Sexuality, Gender, and the Body in Late Medieval Spirituality: Cases from Germany and the Netherlands," *Journal of Feminist Studies in Religion* 7 (spring 1991): 40.

4. HILDEGARD OF BINGEN ON SATISFYING WORK

1. Quoted in Gottfried and Theodoric, *The Life of Holy Hildegard*, trans. James McGrath et al., ed. Mary Palmquist (Collegeville, Minn.: Liturgical Press, 1995), 104.

2. Quotations from Hildegard's texts are cited in the text with the abbreviations listed below. Quotations from *Scivias* include the book number, vision number, and section number from the text. Quotations from the *Book of the Rewards of Life* include the part number and section number. Quotations from the *Book of Divine Works* contain the vision number followed by the section number.

D: *Hildegard of Bingen's Book of Divine Works with Letters and Songs*, ed. Matthew Fox (Santa Fe: Bear and Company, 1987).

R: *The Book of the Rewards of Life (Liber Vitae Meritorum)*, trans. Bruce Hozeski (New York: Oxford University Press, 1994).

SC: *Hildegard of Bingen: Scivias*, trans. Mother Columba Hart and Jane Bishop (New York: Paulist Press, 1990).

3. Caroline Bynum, preface to *Hildegard of Bingen: Scivias*, trans. Mother Columba Hart and Jane Bishop (New York: Paulist Press, 1990), 5.

4. Quoted in Gillian Ahlgren, "Visions and Rhetorical Strategy in the Letters of Hildegard of Bingen," in *Dear Sister: Medieval Women and the Epistolary Genre*, ed. Karen Cherewatuk and Ulrike Wiethaus (Philadelphia: University of Pennsylvania Press, 1993), 49.

5. Quoted in Gottfried and Theodoric, *The Life of Holy Hildegard*, 101.

6. Sabina Flanagan, *Hildegard of Bingen, 1098–1179: A Visionary Life* (New York: Routledge, 1990), 213.

7. Elisabeth Gössmann, "Ipsa enim quasi dumus sapientiae: The Philosophical Anthropology of Hildegard of Bingen," *Mystics Quarterly* 13 (September 1987): 151.

8. Heinrich Schipperges, *Hildegard of Bingen: Healing and the Nature of the Cosmos*, trans. John A. Broadwin (Princeton, N.J.: Markus Wiener Publishers, 1997), 93.

9. Fiona Bowie and Oliver Davies, eds., *Hildegard of Bingen: An Anthology*, trans. Robert Carver (New York: Crossroad, 1990), 30.

10. Barbara Newman, *Sister of Wisdom: St. Hildegard's Theology of the Feminine* (Berkeley: University of California Press, 1987), 251.

11. Ibid., 159.

12. Rosemary Radford Ruether, *Women and Redemption: A Theological History* (Minneapolis: Fortress Press, 1998), 88–90.

13. Barbara Newman, "Some Medieval Theologians and the Sophia Tradition," *The Downside Review* 108 (April 1990): 119.

14. Barbara Newman, *Sister of Wisdom*, 17.

15. Robert Olson, "The Green Man in Hildegard of Bingen," *Studia Mystica* 15 (winter 1992): 12.

16. Quoted in Fiona Bowie and Oliver Davies, eds., *Hildegard of Bingen: An Anthology*, 32; Robert Olson, "The Green Man in Hildegard of Bingen," 14; Constant Mews, "The Virgin, the Apocalypse, and the Exegetical Tradition," in *Wisdom Which Encircles Circles: Papers on Hildegard of Bingen*, ed. Audrey Ekdahl Davidson (Kalamazoo: Medieval Institute Publications, 1996), 34.

17. Rita Brock, "The Greening of the Soul: A Feminist Theological Paradigm of the Web of Life," in *Setting the Table: Women in Theological Conversation*, 133.

5. MARGERY KEMPE ON SEARCHING FOR THE SATISFIED LIFE

1. Margery Kempe, *The Book of Margery Kempe*, trans. B. A. Windeatt (New York: Penguin Books, 1985). Quotations are cited parenthetically in the text and include references to the book number followed by the chapter number. For the best translation in the original English see *The Book of Margery Kempe*, ed. Sanford Brown Meech and Hope Emily Allen (Oxford: Oxford University Press, 1940).

2. For an excellent study of affective piety in the fifteenth century see Clarissa Atkinson, *Mystic and Pilgrim: The Book and the World of Margery Kempe* (Ithaca, N.Y.: Cornell University Press, 1983). Sandra McEntire outlines the history of affective piety. See "The Doctrine of Compunction from Bede to Margery Kempe," in *The Medieval Mystical Tradition in England: Exeter Symposium IV*, ed. Marion Glasscoe (Cambridge: D. S. Brewer, 1987), 77–90.

3. Ellen Ross, *The Grief of God: Images of the Suffering Jesus in Late Medieval England* (New York: Oxford University Press, 1997), 33. In addition to Ross's important study of Kempe, I am indebted to Sandra McEntire's insightful study of the spiritual journey of Margery Kempe. See "The Journey into Selfhood: Margery Kempe and Feminine Spirituality," in *Margery Kempe: A Book of Essays*, ed. Sandra McEntire (New York: Garland, 1992), 51–69.

4. Lynn Staley, *Margery Kempe's Dissenting Fictions* (University Park: Pennsylvania State University Press, 1994), 64.

5. Gunnel Cleve, "Semantic Dimensions in Margery Kempe's 'Whyght Clothys,'" *Mystics Quarterly* 12 (December 1986): 169. Atkinson describes white clothes as an expression of the singularity of Kempe's calling. See *Mystic and Pilgrim*, 51.

6. Atkinson, *Mystic and Pilgrim*, 57.

7. Susan Dickman, "Margery Kempe and the English Devotional Tradition," in *The Medieval Mystical Tradition in England: Exeter Symposium, July 1980*, ed. Marion Glasscoe (Exeter, U.K.: University of Exeter, 1980), 169–70.

8. Karma Lochrie, *Margery Kempe and Translations of the Flesh* (Philadelphia: University of Pennsylvania Press, 1991), 151.

9. McEntire, "Journey into Selfhood," 60.

10. Dhira Mahoney, "Margery Kempe's Tears and the Power over Language," in *Margery Kempe: A Book of Essays*, 47–49.

11. See Atkinson, *Mystic and Pilgrim*, 196–99.

12. Ross, *Grief of God*, 137–38; Atkinson, *Mystic and Pilgrim*, 219–20. Lochrie concludes, "I find Kempe's behavior undesirable as a feminist practice in the twentieth century." See *Translations of Flesh*, 9. On the other hand, Elona Lucas suggests Kempe is a model for Christian living in the material world. See "Poustinia and the 'Worldly' Spirituality of Margery Kempe," *Studia Mystica* 14 (summer/fall 1991): 61.

13. William Provost, "Margery Kempe and Her Calling," in *Margery Kempe: A Book of Essays*, 14.

14. Elizabeth Psakis Armstrong, "'Understanding by Feeling' in Margery Kempe's Book," in *Margery Kempe: A Book of Essays*, 23.

6. HADEWIJCH OF BRABANT ON SERVICE
IN THE SATISFIED LIFE

1. Paul Mommaers, preface to *Hadewijch: The Complete Works*, trans. Mother Columba Hart (Mahwah, N.J.: Paulist Press, 1980), xiii.

2. Elizabeth Wainwright-deKadt, "Courtly Literature and Mysticism: Some Aspects of Their Interaction," *Acta Germanica* 12 (1980): 46.

3. Quotations of Hadewijch's texts are cited in the text with the abbreviations listed below. All quotations are from *Hadewijch: The Complete Works*, trans. Mother Columba Hart (Mahwah, N.J.: Paulist Press, 1980). Quotations for letters and visions include letter number and paragraph number as cited in the Paulist Press edition. Quotations for the Stanza Poems include poem and verse number. Quotations for the Poems in Couplets include poem followed by line number.

> *L:* Letters
> *V:* Visions
> *PS:* Poems in Stanzas
> *PC:* Poems in Couplets

4. Elizabeth Dreyer, *Passionate Women: Two Medieval Mystics* (New York: Paulist Press, 1989), 67.

5. Saskia Murk-Jansen, "The Use of Gender and Gender-Related Imagery in Hadewijch," in *Gender and Text in the Later Middle Ages,* ed. Jane Chance (Gainesville: University Press of Florida, 1996), 64. Murk-Jansen suggests that for Hadewijch the work of salvation is a war on the devil. The crucifixion is capture by the enemy, and this suggests a warlike situation in which the Lord can demand service of the liege knight.

6. Ulrike Wiethaus, "Learning as Experiencing Hadewijch's Model of Spiritual Growth," in *Faith Seeking Understanding: Learning and the Catholic Tradition,* ed. George Berthold (Manchester: St. Anselm College Press, 1991), 96.

7. Elizabeth Alvilda Petroff, "Gender, Knowledge, and Power in Hadewijch's *Strophische Gedichten,*" in *Body and Soul: Essays on Medieval Women and Mysticism* (New York: Oxford University Press, 1994), 184, 201. Joris Reynaert argues that Love does not represent God but is a personification of God. See "Hadewijch: Mystic Poetry and Courtly Love," in *Medieval Dutch Literature in Its European Context,* ed. Erik Kooper (Cambridge: Cambridge University Press, 1994), 212. Ulrike Wiethaus likens Love to the Hindu goddess Kali as a strong-willed, single-minded, fiery image of the feminine divine. See "Sexuality, Gender, and the Body," 45, 48.

8. Emilie Zum Brunn and Georgette Epiney-Burgard, *Women Mystics in Medieval Europe,* 101.

9. Reynaert, "Mystic Poetry," 214.

10. Don Nugent, "The Harvest of Hadewijch: Brautmystik and Wesenmystik," *Mystics Quarterly* 12 (September 1986): 121.

11. John Giles Milhaven, *Hadewijch and Her Sisters: Other Ways of Loving and Knowing* (Albany: State University of New York Press, 1993), 62.

12. Wiethaus, "Learning," 104.

13. Nugent, "The Harvest of Hadewijch," 125.

14. Milhaven, *Hadewijch and Her Sisters*, 32.

15. Quoted in Odette Baumer-Despeigne, "Hadewijch of Antwerp and Hadewijch II: Mysticism of Being in the Thirteenth Century in Brabant," *Studia Mystica* 14 (winter 1991): 23.

16. Nicholas Watson, "'Classics of Western Spirituality,' II: Three Medieval Women Theologians and Their Background," *King's Theological Review* 12 (autumn 1989): 60. Nugent calls Hadewijch a pyromaniac on fire with the Love of God. See "The Harvest of Hadewijch," 122.

17. Mother Columba Hart, introduction to *Hadewijch: the Complete Works*, trans. Mother Columba Hart (Mahwah, N.J.: Paulist Press, 1980), 37. Sheila Carney suggests that in her awareness of human dignity and human responsibility Hadewijch has a contemporary appeal and provides a model for those "straining to give birth to a just society." See "Exemplarism in Hadewijch: The Quest for Full-Grownness," *The Downside Review* 103 (October 1985): 292, 294. Milhaven suggests Hadewijch (and other medieval mystics) give a fuller account of embodied mutuality than modern feminist scholars. See *Hadewijch and Her Sisters*, 76.

18. Elizabeth Alvilda Petroff, "A New Feminine Spirituality: The Beguines and Their Writings in Medieval Europe," in *Body and Soul*, 61–62. Mary Suydam writes that "the great achievement of Beguine writers in general and of Hadewijch in particular, was the empowering assertion that the experiences of the whole human, and specifically those of the whole woman, are sites for connection with God." See "The Touch of Satisfaction: Visions and the Religious Experience According to Hadewijch of Antwerp," *Journal of Feminist Studies in Religion* 12 (fall 1996): 27.

7. CATHERINE OF SIENA ON SUFFERING OF THE SATISFIED LIFE

1. Caroline Walker Bynum, *Holy Feast and Holy Fast: The Religious Significance of Food to Medieval Women* (Berkeley: University of California Press, 1987), 301.

2. Darby Kathleen Ray, *Deceiving the Devil*, 143.

3. Richard Kieckhefer, *Unquiet Souls: Fourteenth-Century Saints and Their Religious Milieu* (Chicago: University of Chicago Press, 1984), 194–95.

4. Quotations from Catherine's texts and the *Life of Catherine* are cited in the text with the abbreviations listed below. Quotations from the *Life of Catherine* include the part number, chapter number, followed by the section number. Quotations from *The Dialogue* include chapter number. Quotations from *The Prayers* include the prayer number as listed in the edition by Suzanne Noffke. Selections from the *Letters* include the page number of the edition quoted.

L: *The Life of Catherine of Siena* by Raymond of Capua, trans. Conleth Kearns (Wilmington, Del.: Michael Glazier, 1980).

D: *The Dialogue*, trans. Suzanne Noffke (New York: Paulist Press, 1980).

P: *The Prayers of Catherine of Siena*, ed. Suzanne Noffke (New York: Paulist Press, 1983).

LN: *The Letters of Catherine of Siena*, vol. 1, trans. Suzanne Noffke (Binghamton, N.Y.: Center for Medieval and Early Renaissance Studies, 1988).

LP: *Medieval Women's Visionary Literature*, ed. Elizabeth Alvilda Petroff (New York: Oxford University Press, 1986).

LK: *I, Catherine: Selected Writings of St. Catherine of Siena*, by Catherine of Siena, trans. Kenelm Foster and Mary John Ronayne (London: Collins and Co., 1980).

5. Suzanne Noffke, *Catherine of Siena: Vision Through a Distant Eye* (Collegeville, Minn.: Liturgical Press, 1996), 16.

6. Kenelm Foster, Introduction to *I, Catherine: Selected Writings of St. Catherine of Siena*, by Catherine of Siena, trans. Kenelm Foster and Mary John Ronayne (London: Collins and Co., 1980), 29.

7. Linda Mills Woolsey, "Feather, Spark, and Mustard Seed: Hildegard of Bingen and Catherine of Siena," *Daughters of Sarah* 21 (winter 1995): 29.

8. Suzanne Noffke, *The Prayers of Catherine of Siena* (New York: Paulist Press, 1983), 184.

9. Nancy Siraisi, *Medieval and Early Renaissance Medicine: An Introduction to Knowledge and Practice* (Chicago: University of Chicago Press, 1990), 139.

10. Elizabeth Alvilda Petroff, *Medieval Women's Visionary Literature*, 240.

11. For an example of the condemnation of Catherine, see Rudolph Bell, *Holy Anorexia* (Chicago: University of Chicago Press, 1985). For the appraisal of Catherine as a feminist, see Mary Giles, "The Feminist Mystic," in *The Feminist Mystic and Other Essays on Women and Spirituality* (New York: Crossroad, 1982), 6–38. Caroline Bynum and Suzanne Noffke are two of the best scholars in terms of capturing the fullness of the meaning of Catherine's life. See *Holy Feast and Holy Fast*, 165–80, and *Catherine of Siena: Vision through a Distant Eye*.

12. Dorothee Soelle, *Suffering*, trans. Everett Kalin (Philadelphia: Fortress Press, 1975), 108, 125. Soelle suggests that mystical theology has a unique ability to fully understand the true nature of suffering in the Christian life. See 102.

8. BEING AT HOME WITH OURSELVES IN GOD

1. Rosemary Ruether, *Women and Redemption*, 273–75.

2. Mary Daly and Jane Caputi, *Webster's First New Intergalactic Wickedary of the English Language* (Boston: Beacon Press, 1987), 201. Daly defines plastic passions as ideas that mask oppression and drain creative energy. See 217.

BIBLIOGRAPHY

Aers, David, and Lynn Staley. *The Powers of the Holy: Religion, Politics and Gender in Late Medieval English Culture.* University Park: Pennsylvania State University Press, 1996.

Ahlgren, Gillian. "Visions and Rhetorical Strategy in the Letters of Hildegard of Bingen." In *Dear Sister: Medieval Women and the Epistolary Genre,* edited by Karen Cherewatuk and Ulrike Wiethaus. Philadelphia: University of Pennsylvania Press, 1993.

Anderson, Elizabeth. "Mechthild Von Magdeburg: Her Creativity and Her Audience." In *Women, the Book, and the Godly,* vol. 1, edited by Lesley Smith and Jane Taylor. Cambridge: D. S. Brewer, 1995.

Anselm of Canterbury. *Why God Became Man and The Virgin Conception and Original Sin.* Translated by Joseph Colleran. Albany: Magi Books, Inc., 1969.

Armstrong, Elizabeth Psakis. " 'Understanding by Feeling' in Margery Kempe's *Book.*" In *Margery Kempe: A Book of Essays,* edited by Sandra McEntire. New York: Garland Publishing, 1992.

Atkinson, Clarissa. *Mystic and Pilgrim: The Book and the World of Margery Kempe.* Ithaca, N.Y.: Cornell University Press, 1983.

Baker, Denise Nowakowski. *Julian of Norwich's Showings: From Vision to Book.* Princeton, N.J.: Princeton University Press, 1994.

Barratt, Alexandra. "How Many Children Had Julian of Norwich? Editions, Translations, and Versions of Her Revelations." In *Vox Mystica: Essays for Valerie M. Lagorio,* edited by Anne Clark Bartlett et al. Cambridge: D. S. Brewer, 1995.

Baumer-Despeigne, Odette. "Hadewijch of Antwerp and Hadewijch II: Mysticism of Being in the Thirteenth Century in Brabant." *Studia Mystica* 14 (winter 1991): 16–37.

Bell, Rudolph. *Holy Anorexia.* Chicago: University of Chicago Press, 1985.

Bondi, Roberta C. *Memories of God: Theological Reflections on a Life*. Nashville: Abingdon, 1995.

Bowie, Fiona, and Oliver Davies, eds. *Hildegard of Bingen: An Anthology*. Translated by Robert Carver. London: SPCK, 1990.

Bozak-DeLeo, Lillian. "The Soteriology of Julian of Norwich." In *Theology and the University*, edited by John Apczynski. Lanham, Md.: University Press of America, 1987.

Bradley, Ritamary. "Two Excerpts from *Julian's Way*." *Mystics Quarterly* 18 (September 1992): 75–81.

Brock, Rita. "The Greening of the Soul: A Feminist Theological Paradigm of the Web of Life." In *Setting the Table: Women in Theological Conversation*, edited by Rita Nakashima Brock, Claudia Camp, and Serene Jones. St. Louis: Chalice Press, 1995.

Brown, Joanne Carlson. "Divine Child Abuse?" *Daughters of Sarah* 18 (summer 1992): 24–28.

Brümmer, Vincent. "Atonement and Reconciliation." *Religious Studies* 28 (December 1992): 435–52.

Brunn, Emilie Zum, and Georgette Epiney-Burgard. *Women Mystics in Medieval Europe*. Translated by Sheila Hughes. New York: Paragon House, 1989.

Bynum, Caroline Walker. *Holy Feast and Holy Fast: The Religious Significance of Food to Medieval Women*. Berkeley: University of California Press, 1987.

———. *Jesus as Mother: Studies in the Spirituality of the High Middle Ages*. Berkeley: University of California Press, 1982.

———. Preface to *Hildegard of Bingen: Scivias*. Translated by Mother Columba Hart and Jane Bishop. New York: Paulist Press, 1990.

Carney, Sheila. "Exemplarism in Hadewijch: The Quest for Full-Grownness." *Downside Review* 103 (October 1985): 276–95.

Catherine of Siena. *I, Catherine: Selected Writings of St. Catherine of Siena*. Translated by Kenelm Foster and Mary John Ronayne. London: Collins and Co., 1980.

———. *The Dialogue*. Translated by Suzanne Noffke. New York: Paulist Press, 1980.

———. *The Letters of Catherine of Siena*. Vol. 1. Translated by Suzanne Noffke. Binghamton, N.Y.: Center for Medieval and Early Renaissance Studies, 1988.

———. *The Prayers of Catherine of Siena*. Edited by Suzanne Noffke. New York: Paulist Press, 1983.

Clark, J. P. H. "Time and Eternity in Julian of Norwich." *Downside Review* 109 (October 1991): 259–76.

Clark, Susan. "'Ze Glicher Wis'": Mechthild von Magdeburg and the Concept of Likeness." In *The Worlds of Medieval Women: Creativity, Influence, Imagination*, edited by Constance Berman et al. Morgantown: West Virginia University Press, 1985.

Cleve, Gunnel. "Semantic Dimensions in Margery Kempe's 'Whyght Clothys.'" *Mystics Quarterly* 12 (December 1986): 162–70.

Corless, Roger. "The Dramas of Spiritual Progress: The Lord and the Servant in Julian's Showings 51 and the Lost Heir in Lotus Sutra 4." *Mystics Quarterly* 11 (June 1985): 65–75.

Daly, Mary. *Beyond God the Father: Toward a Philosophy of Women's Liberation.* Boston: Beacon Press, 1973.

————, and Jane Caputi. *Webster's First New Intergalactic Wickedary of the English Language.* Boston: Beacon Press, 1987.

Davies, Oliver. "Transformational Processes in the Work of Julian of Norwich and Mechthild of Magdeburg." In *The Medieval Mystical Tradition in England: Exeter Symposium V,* edited by Marion Glasscoe. Cambridge: D. S. Brewer, 1992.

Dickman, Susan. "Margery Kempe and the English Devotional Tradition." In *The Medieval Mystical Tradition in England: Exeter Symposium, July 1980,* edited by Marion Glasscoe. Exeter, U.K.: University of Exeter, 1980.

Dreyer, Elizabeth. *Passionate Women: Two Medieval Mystics.* New York: Paulist Press, 1989.

Fiddes, Paul. *Past Event and Present Salvation: The Christian Idea of Atonement.* Louisville: Westminster/John Knox Press, 1989.

Flanagan, Sabina. *Hildegard of Bingen, 1098–1179: A Visionary Life.* New York: Routledge, 1990.

Foster, Kenelm. Introduction to *I, Catherine: Selected Writings of St Catherine of Siena,* by Catherine of Siena, translated by Kenelm Foster and Mary John Ronayne. London: Collins and Co., 1980.

Giles, Mary. "The Feminist Mystic." In *The Feminist Mystic and Other Essays on Women and Spirituality.* New York: Crossroad, 1982.

Gorringe, Timothy. *Redeeming Time: Atonement through Education.* London: Darton, Longman, and Todd, 1986.

Gössmann, Elisabeth. "Ipsa enim quasi domus sapientiae: The Philosophical Anthropology of Hildegard of Bingen." *Mystics Quarterly* 13 (September 1987): 146–54.

Gottfried and Theoderic. *The Life of the Holy Hildegard.* Translated by James McGrath et al. Edited by Mary Palmquist. Collegeville, Minn.: Liturgical Press, 1995.

Grey, Mary. *Feminism, Redemption, and Christian Tradition.* Mystic, Conn.: Twenty-Third Publications, 1990.

Hadewijch. *Hadewijch: The Complete Works.* Translated by Mother Columba Hart. Mahwah, N.J.: Paulist Press, 1980.

Hancock, Maxine. "Mysticism, Dissidence, and Didacticism: Recovering the Tradition of Women Writing the Faith, 1350–1800." *Crux* 32 (June 1996): 20–29.

Hart, Mother Columba. Introduction to *Hadewijch: The Complete Works,* by Hadewijch, translated by Mother Columba Hart. Mahwah, N.J.: Paulist Press, 1980.

Hay, Louise. *You Can Heal Your Life.* Santa Monica, Calif.: Hay House, 1987.

Hildegard of Bingen. *Hildegard of Bingen's Book of Divine Works with Letters and Songs.* Edited by Matthew Fox. Santa Fe: Bear and Company, 1987.

————. *The Book of the Rewards of Life (Liber Vitae Meritorum)*. Translated by Bruce Hozeski. New York: Oxford University Press, 1994.

————. *Hildegard of Bingen: Scivias*. Translated by Mother Columba Hart and Jane Bishop. New York: Paulist Press, 1990.

Hollywood, Amy. *The Soul as Virgin Wife: Mechthild of Magdeburg, Marguerite Porete, and Meister Eckhart*. Notre Dame, Ind.: University of Notre Dame Press, 1996.

Jantzen, Grace M. *Julian of Norwich: Mystic and Theologian*. New York: Paulist Press, 1988.

Julian of Norwich. *Showings*. Translated by Edmund Colledge and James Walsh. New York: Paulist Press, 1978.

Kempe, Margery. *The Book of Margery Kempe*. Translated by B. A. Windeatt. New York: Penguin Books, 1985.

————. *The Book of Margery Kempe*. Edited by Sanford Brown Meech and Hope Emily Allen. Oxford: Oxford University Press, 1940.

Lahutsky, Nadia. "Food and Feminism and Historical Interpretations: The Case of Medieval Holy Women." In *Setting the Table: Women in Theological Conversation*, edited by Rita Nakashima Brock, Claudia Camp, and Serene Jones. St. Louis: Chalice Press, 1995.

Lichtmann, Maria R. "'I desyrede a bodylye sight': Julian of Norwich and the Body." *Mystics Quarterly* 17 (March 1991): 12–19.

————. "Julian of Norwich and the Ontology of the Feminine." *Studia Mystica* 13 (March 1990): 53–65.

Lochrie, Karma. *Margery Kempe and Translations of the Flesh*. Philadelphia: University of Pennsylvania Press, 1991.

Lucas, Elona. "Poustinia and the 'Worldly' Spirituality of Margery Kempe." *Studia Mystica* 14 (summer/fall 1991): 61–71.

Maimela, Simon. "The Atonement in the Context of Liberation Theology." *Journal of Theology for Southern Africa* 39 (June 1982): 45–54.

Marshall, Molly. "On a Hill Too Far Away?: Reclaiming the Cross as the Critical Interpretive Principle of the Christian Life." *Review and Expositor* 91 (spring 1994): 247–59.

McEntire, Sandra. "The Doctrine of Compunction from Bede to Margery Kempe." In *The Medieval Mystical Tradition in England: Exeter Symposium IV*, edited by Marion Glasscoe. Cambridge: D. S. Brewer, 1987.

————. "Journey into Selfhood: Margery Kempe and Feminine Spirituality." In *Margery Kempe: A Book of Essays*, edited by Sandra McEntire. New York: Garland Publishing, 1992.

McFague, Sallie. *Models of God: Theology for an Ecological, Nuclear Age*. Philadelphia: Fortress Press, 1987.

McGinn, Bernard, ed. *Meister Eckhart and the Beguine Mystics: Hadewijch of Brabant, Mechthild of Magdeburg, and Marguerite Porete*. New York: Continuum, 1994.

Mechthild of Magdeburg. *The Flowing Light of the Godhead*. Translated by Frank Tobin. Preface by Margot Schmidt. New York: Paulist Press, 1997.

Menzies, Lucy. Introduction to *The Revelations of Mechthild of Magdeburg (1200–1297) or The Flowing Light of the Godhead*, translated by Lucy Menzies. London: Longman, Green, and Co., 1953.

Mews, Constant. "The Virgin, the Apocalypse, and the Exegetical Tradition." In *Wisdom Which Encircles Circles*, edited by Audrey Ekdahl Davidson. Kalamazoo: Medieval Institute Publications, 1996.

Milhaven, John Giles. *Hadewijch and Her Sisters: Other Ways of Loving and Knowing*. Albany: State University of New York Press, 1993.

Mommaers, Paul. Preface to *Hadewijch: The Complete Works*, by Hadewijch, translated by Mother Columba Hart. Mahwah, N.J.: Paulist Press, 1980.

Murk-Jansen, Saskia. "The Use of Gender and Gender-Related Imagery in Hadewijch." In *Gender and Text in the Later Middle Ages*, edited by Jane Chance. Gainesville: University Press of Florida, 1996.

Newman, Barbara. *Sister of Wisdom: St. Hildegard's Theology of the Feminine*. Berkeley: University of California Press, 1987.

———. "Some Mediaeval Theologians and the Sophia Tradition." *Downside Review* 108 (April 1990): 111–30.

Noffke, Suzanne. *Catherine of Siena: Vision Through a Distant Eye*. Collegeville, Minn.: Liturgical Press, 1996.

Nugent, Don. "The Harvest of Hadewijch: Brautmystik and Wesenmystik." *Mystics Quarterly* 12 (September 1986): 119–26.

Nuth, Joan. "Two Medieval Soteriologies: Anselm of Canterbury and Julian of Norwich." *Theological Studies* 53 (December 1992): 611–45.

Olson, Mary. "God's Inappropriate Grace: Images of Courtesy in Julian of Norwich's Showings." *Mystics Quarterly* 20 (June 1994): 47–59.

Olson, Robert. "The Green Man in Hildegard of Bingen." *Studia Mystica* 15 (winter 1992): 3–18.

Pelphrey, Brant. *Christ Our Mother: Julian of Norwich*. Wilmington, Del.: Michael Glazier, 1989.

Peters, Brad. "Julian of Norwich and the Internalized Dialogue of Prayer." *Mystics Quarterly* 20 (December 1994): 122–30.

Peters, Ted. "Atonement and the Final Scapegoat." *Perspectives in Religious Studies* 19 (summer 1992): 151–81.

Petroff, Elizabeth Alvilda. "Gender, Knowledge, and Power in Hadewijch's *Strophische Gedichten*." In *Body and Soul: Essays on Medieval Women and Mysticism*. New York: Oxford University Press, 1994.

———. "A New Feminine Spirituality: The Beguines and Their Writings in Medieval

Europe." In *Body and Soul: Essays on Medieval Women and Mysticism*. New York: Oxford University Press, 1994.

————, ed. *Medieval Women's Visionary Literature*. New York: Oxford University Press, 1986.

Phillips, Helen. "Rewriting the Fall: Julian of Norwich and the *Chevaliers des Dames*." In *Women, the Book and the Godly: Selected Proceedings of the St. Hilda's Conference*, vol. 1, edited by Lesley Smith and Jane H. M. Taylor. Cambridge: D. S. Brewer, 1995.

Pitino, Rick. *Success Is a Choice: 10 Steps to Overachieving in Business and Life*. New York: Broadway Books, 1997.

Provost, William. "Margery Kempe and Her Calling." In *Margery Kempe: A Book of Essays*, edited by Sandra McEntire. New York: Garland Publishing, 1992.

Putnam, Johnette. "Mechthild of Magdeburg: Poet and Mystic." In *Medieval Women Monastics: Wisdom's Wellsprings*, edited by Miriam Schmitt and Linda Kulzer. Collegeville, Minn.: Liturgical Press, 1996.

Ray, Darby Kathleen. *Deceiving the Devil: Atonement, Abuse, and Ransom*. Cleveland: The Pilgrim Press, 1998.

Ray, Inna Jane. "The Atonement Muddle: An Historical Analysis and Clarification of a Salvation Theory." *Journal of Women and Religion* 15 (1997): 12–135.

Raymond of Capua. *The Life of Catherine of Siena*. Translated by Conleth Kearns. Wilmington, Del.: Michael Glazier, 1980.

Reynaert, Joris. "Hadewijch: Mystic Poetry and Courtly Love." In *Medieval Dutch Literature in Its European Context*, edited by Erik Kooper. Cambridge: Cambridge University Press, 1994.

Robertson, Elizabeth. "Medieval Medical Views of Women and Female Spirituality in the *Ancrene Wise* and Julian of Norwich's *Showings*." In *Feminist Approaches to the Body in Medieval Literature*, edited by Linda Lomperis and Sarah Stanbury. Philadelphia: University of Pennsylvania Press, 1993.

Ross, Ellen. *The Grief of God: Images of the Suffering Jesus in Late Medieval England*. New York: Oxford University Press, 1997.

Ruether, Rosemary Radford. *Women and Redemption: A Theological History*. Minneapolis: Fortress Press, 1998.

Saiving, Valerie. "The Human Situation: A Feminine View." *Journal of Religion* 40 (April 1960): 100–12.

Schaller, Janet. "Mentoring of Women: Transformation in Adult Religious Education." *Religious Education* 91 (spring 1996): 160–71.

Schipperges, Heinrich. *Hildegard of Bingen: Healing and the Nature of the Cosmos*. Princeton, N.J.: Markus Wiener Publishers, 1997.

Seaton, William. "Transformation of Convention in Mechthild of Magdeburg." *Mystics Quarterly* 10 (June 1984): 64–72.

Siraisi, Nancy. *Medieval and Early Renaissance Medicine: An Introduction to Knowledge and Practice*. Chicago: University of Chicago Press, 1990.

Soelle, Dorothee. *Suffering*. Translated by Everett Kalin. Philadelphia: Fortress Press, 1975.

Solberg, Mary. *Compelling Knowledge: A Feminist Proposal for an Epistemology of the Cross*. Albany: State University of New York Press, 1997.

Sprung, Andrew. "'We nevyr shall come out of hyin': Enclosure and Immanence in Julian of Norwich's *Book of Showings*." *Mystics Quarterly* 19 (June 1993): 47–62.

Staley, Lynn. "Julian of Norwich and the Late Fourteenth-Century Crisis of Authority." In *The Power of the Holy: Religion, Politics, and Gender in Late Medieval English Culture*, edited by David Aers and Lynn Staley. University Park: Pennsylvania State University Press, 1996.

———. *Margery Kempe's Dissenting Fictions*. University Park: Pennsylvania State University Press, 1994.

Suydam, Mary. "The Touch of Satisfaction: Visions and the Religious Experience According to Hadewijch of Antwerp." *Journal of Feminist Studies in Religion* 12 (fall 1996): 5–28.

Van Dyk, Leanne. "Do Theories of Atonement Foster Abuse?" *Dialog* 35 (winter 1996): 21–25.

Wainwright-deKadt, Elizabeth. "Courtly Literature and Mysticism: Some Aspects of Their Interaction." *Acta Germanica* 12 (1980): 41–60.

Watson, Nicholas. "'Classics of Western Spirituality,' II: Three Medieval Women Theologians and Their Background." *King's Theological Review* 12 (autumn 1989): 56–64.

Wiethaus, Ulrike. "Learning as Experiencing Hadewijch's Model of Spiritual Growth." In *Faith Seeking Understanding: Learning and the Catholic Tradition*, edited by George Berthold. Manchester: St. Anselm College Press, 1991.

———. "Sexuality, Gender, and the Body in Late Medieval Spirituality: Cases from Germany and the Netherlands." *Journal of Feminist Studies in Religion* 7 (spring 1991): 35–52.

———. "Suffering, Love, and Transformation in Mechthild of Magdeburg." *Listening* 22 (spring 1987): 139–50.

Williams, Delores. "Black Women's Surrogacy Experience and the Christian Notion of Redemption." In *After Patriarchy: Feminist Transformations of the World Religions*, edited by Paula Cooey, William Eakin, and Jay McDaniel. Maryknoll, N.Y.: Orbis Books, 1991.

Woolsey, Linda Mills. "Feather, Spark, and Mustard Seed: Hildegard of Bingen and Catherine of Siena." *Daughters of Sarah* 21 (winter 1995): 28–31.

Young, Pamela Dickey. "Beyond Moral Influence to an Atoning Life." *Theology Today* 52 (October 1995): 344–55.

INDEX

Abelard, 5
Aers, David, 22
anchoress, 11–12, 66–67, 79
Anselm, critique of, 14–16, 25, 60; and
    Hadewijch, 89, 97; and Hildegard, 60;
    and Julian, 19
Armstrong, Elizabeth, 81
Atkinson, Clarissa, 79
atonement: classical theory, 5; definition,
    ix, 1, 25, 43, 118; objective theory,
    15; subjective theory, 27. *See also*
    Anselm; salvation

Baker, Denise, 11
beguines, 29–30, 67, 84–87
Bondi, Roberta, 3, 5, 6, 12, 16, 41–42, 113
Brock, Rita, 59
Brown, Joanne Carlson, 2
Brümmer, Vincent, 15
Brunn, Emilie Zum, 41

Catherine: and blood symbolism, 106,
    111, 115; and critics, 101, 102, 112;
and fasting, 101–2, 104, 108, 114;
    and Hadewijch, 112; and Hildegard,
    115; and Julian, 113, 115; and
    Margery Kempe, 112; and obedience,
    106; and prayer, 110–11, 113; and
    Raymond of Capua, 101–2; and
    self-concept, 108, 113
Christ, 118; as bridge, 106; crucifixion
    of, 1–3, 14, 26, 40, 53–55, 115; as
    gardener, 22, 27; incarnation of,
    26, 52; as light, 52; Margery Kempe
    as mother of, 77; as mother, 22–23;
    as servant (second Adam), 21; as
    substitution, 88; and suffering, 38,
    76, 97, 109
communion (Eucharist), 3–4, 118–19;
    and Catherine, 109–10; and Julian,
    22–23; and Hadewijch, 93; and
    Hildegard, 53
courtly love: and Julian, 19; and
    Hadewijch, 85, 89, 95; and
    Mechthild, 30, 33, 35. *See also* love
    mysticism